Eliminating Racial Profiling in School Discipline

Cultures in Conflict

Martha R. Bireda

A SCARECROWEDUCATION BOOK

The Scarecrow Press, Inc.
Lanham, Maryland, and London
2002

A SCARECROWEDUCATION BOOK

Published in the United States of America
by Scarecrow Press, Inc.
A Member of the Rowman & Littlefield Publishing Group
4720 Boston Way, Lanham, Maryland 20706
www.scarecrowpress.com

4 Pleydell Gardens, Folkstone
Kent CT20 2DN, England

British Library Cataloguing in Publication Information Available

Library of Congress Cataloging-in-Publication Data

Bireda, Martha R.
    Eliminating racial profiling in school discipline : cultures in conflict / Martha R. Bireda.
    p. cm.
    ISBN 0-8108-4201-7 (alk. paper)
    1. School discipline—United States. 2. Discrimination in education—United States. I.
Title.

    LB3012.2 .B57 2002
    371.5'8—dc21

                  2001048325

♾️™ The paper used in this publication meets the minimum requirements of American
National Standard for Information Sciences—Permanence of Paper for Printed Library
Materials, ANSI/NISO Z39.48-1992.
Manufactured in the United States of America.

Dedicated to African American male students,
who, because they are feared and misunderstood,
are denied equal educational opportunity.

Contents

Foreword

Nearly fifty years after the *Brown v. Board of Education* decision called for the desegregation of schools, we find that the residue of discrimination still lingers in our halls of learning. This discrimination includes an over-representation of African Americans in our special education classes, and an under-representation of minorities in the gifted classes. Or if we collected data by race, we would find that test scores and achievement scores of these same students are significantly lower, dropout rates and placement in alternative schools are higher, graduation rates are lower, and success and hope are hard to find.

Across the country, the most pervasive face of discrimination in our schools can be seen in the disparate numbers of African American students, mostly male, that are disciplined and suspended from our schools, often unable to recover. If educators question these numbers, they would have to look beyond the symptomatic behaviors, test scores, and grades they see to understand the underlying reasons our minority students are failing in our schools.

Perhaps our schools are failing our African American students. Perhaps our educational institutions have failed to understand the culture of all of our children or the diversity of their needs. Perhaps we have not created inviting school climates, where teachers are prepared to understand the background and needs of our African American students, or indeed, all of our minority students. Yet we find ourselves in an age when educators are striving to "leave no child behind." Dr. Bireda has researched and studied this phenomena of disparate numbers of African American males disciplined and suspended in our schools. She has searched beyond the symptomatic behaviors and disturbing numbers so that educators might better understand the reasons for these disproportionate numbers and thus give them the ability to examine responses to the students that have been left behind in ways that are more appropriate and educationally sound. Martha, additionally, provides ways administrators and teachers can create a culturally sensitive environment for those at-risk students left behind. Dr. Bireda's vast educational and cultural experiences as well as her extensive background in counseling serve her well in this publication and make us all richer for the experience of reading it.

Nancy L. Peck, Ed.D.
Director, Southeastern Equity Center
Miami, Florida

Acknowledgments

A very special thanks to:

Dr. Nancy Peck, for encouraging me to write about the racial disparity in school discipline. Dr. Peck's dedicated work in the equity field for more than thirty years has been an inspiration to me.

Dr. Donna Elam, Tery Medina, Grace Reyes, and Michele Boucicaut, for being the wonderfully helpful and supportive colleagues that they are.

Dawn Spivey, who through our many talks on travels to school districts became my "muse."

Dr. J. Vann Sikes, Mr. Jay Brinson, and the talented members of the Superintendent's Advisory Committee in Crisp County, Georgia, for permission to use their excellent materials in this publication.

The Atlanta Office of Civil Rights for generously providing discipline statistics.

Julia Potter of WEEA for her suggestions and encouragement.

The many students and parents who over the years have shared their stories, and enabled me to have real insight into the problem of racial disparity in school discipline; especially the parent group and their advisor, Mrs. Betty Dunlap, from Harris County, Georgia.

DØ73Ø632

Introduction

This book had its genesis almost ten years ago, when an African American principal requested that I visit his middle school in a small, Southern school district. He was concerned that he and his office were being inundated with discipline referrals for African American students, especially males. He showed me files filled with referrals, most of which he felt were unwarranted. I spent three days at the school, talking to parents, teachers, and students. My plan was to conduct a workshop for teachers after gathering information from the three groups. The students who were sent to me (not specifically at my request) turned out to be the "problem" students. It was early in the second semester of school, and some of the students in the group had received as many as fifty-plus referrals to the principal's office. The students whom I talked to that day and the students who had been described to me by teachers appeared to be two entirely different groups. I talked to a group of students who honestly and openly admitted that they misbehaved, but also expressed a great deal of anger and pain. There was one young man, however, a tall, rather heavyset youngster who appeared to be older than his actual age, who touched me deeply.

In fact, I will never forget the sadness in his eyes and the pain in his voice when he responded to my inquiry as to why he had so many referrals. With a great deal of respect to me, he said, "Ma'am, if you were in my shoes for one day, how would you react?" That day, I started to really listen to students, especially the "bad kids," and to hear their experiences and their pain.

After that experience, I designed a workshop for administrators and teachers to help reduce the number of disciplinary referrals for African American students, especially males. It was not until 2000, almost ten years later, that everything I felt as an educator, counselor, and equity consultant was affirmed. Three national studies confirmed that there is more to the racial disparity in discipline than meets the eye. These studies provided the data that left no doubt that we as teachers and administrators must look more closely at the school climate, teacher–student relationships, and the in-school experiences of African American students if we are to drastically reduce the disproportionate numbers of disciplinary referrals and sanctions for African American students.

This book is designed to provide administrators and teachers with knowledge of behaviors and precipitating factors that increase the potential for African American students, especially male students, to be referred for disciplinary actions. Specifically, the reader will gain an awareness of the *culturally influenced* communication style of African American male students that often contributes to tension in classroom interactions with their teachers. In addition, the reader will become aware of the *culturally conditioned* beliefs and assumptions about African American students, especially males, that affect teacher–student rapport and relationships. Finally, this book provides teachers and administrators with a set of strategies that can be utilized to reduce the high frequency of disciplinary referrals and actions involving African American students. A majority of teachers are white and female; this book can be of particular assistance in helping them to better understand the culturally based and culturally conditioned factors that influence disciplinary incidents involving African American male students. This book will also be beneficial to African American and other teachers who may desire to better understand how the social class of the teacher and student has an influence on the student–teacher interaction and disciplinary incidents. In part 1 of the book, I examine *system-related factors* that contribute to the racial disparities in discipline. In chapter 1, an overview of current research data related to racial disproportionality in discipline is presented; in chapter 2, factors that are the by-products of institutional racism and that place African American students, especially males, at risk for disciplinary actions are discussed. Part 2 addresses the influence of *culturally based* and *culturally conditioned* factors on classroom interactions between the African American student and his teachers. Chapter 3 deals with the impact of the African American student's culture; chapter 4 specially addresses communication differences that can be problematic in the classroom; chapter 5 explores the impact of conscious and unconscious stereotyping of the African American male in particular; and chapter 6 describes how cultural conflicts and stereotyping lead to inequities in the classroom. In part 3, strategies for creating culturally respective and accepting classroom environments for African American students, as well as for eliminating disparities in discipline referrals and sanctions, will be provided. Specific strategies for the administrator's role of changing the school climate (chapter 7); changing individual attitudes (chapter 8); working with parents and the community (chapter 9); and evaluating the process (chapter 10) are discussed.

The ultimate goal of this book is to contribute to the increased academic achievement of African American students. African American students who are sitting in the office (with nothing to do), in in-school suspension, out of school without the benefit of instruction, or placed in inadequate alternative educational settings cannot and will not experience academic success. As we enter the twenty-first century, it is urgent that we as educators reach out to all students, and find new ways to ensure that they have positive, successful experiences, and remain in school until graduation.

Workshops

Dr. Bireda offers workshops for administrators, teachers, and parents related to discipline and achievement issues affecting minority students.

If you would like to receive information about these workshops, please contact:

> The Bireda Group
> P.O. Box 510818
> Punta Gorda, FL 33951-0818
> Email: biredagrp@aol.com

PART I

CHAPTER 1

Discipline: The New Equity Issue

Almost fifty years after *Brown v. Board of Education*, racial inequity continues to be a serious problem in U.S. public schools. A student's race and color are still significant arbiters of his or her school experiences, opportunities, and academic success. A study conducted by the Applied Research Center (2000) found a preponderance of statistical evidence pointing to glaring racial inequities and discrimination in U.S. public schools. The study revealed that students of color have less access to advanced classes or programs for gifted students and that students of color are more likely to drop out of school and are less likely to graduate than White students. Discipline—disproportional, extreme, and unwarranted—has become the new tool for depriving African American students of equal educational opportunity. Whether deliberate or unintentional, African American students, particularly males, are trapped in a vicious cycle that leads to their resegregation from the main school population, placement in alternative programs that don't adequately address their educational needs, and the increased likelihood of dropping out. The magnitude of the problem is evidenced by several recent national studies and by Office of Civil Rights reports. Researchers from the Advancement Project and the Civil Rights Project at Harvard University (2000) found that:

- Black students represent 17 percent of enrollment nationally, but 32 percent of out-of-school suspensions.
- Black children, particularly Black males, are disciplined more often and more severely than any other minority group.

3

- Almost 25 percent of all Black male students were suspended at least once over a four-year period.
- Zero-tolerance policies are more likely to exist in predominately Black and Latino school districts.
- Black and Latino students are more likely to be referred for disciplinary action and to be disciplined.
- Black and Latino students are more likely to be disciplined for minor conduct and to receive punishments disproportionate to their conduct.
- Black and Latino students tend to be suspended for discretionary offenses, such as "defiance of authority" and "disrespect of authority."

These categories of conduct provide latitude for racial bias to affect discipline actions.

Skiba and others (2000) tested alternative hypotheses for disproportionate school discipline and found that:

- Racial and gender discrepancies in school disciplinary outcomes were consistent regardless of methodology.
- There is no evidence that racial disparities disappear when controlling for poverty status.
- There is no evidence that Black students act out more than other students of different racial backgrounds.
- Disproportionate representation of Black students in office referrals, suspensions, and expulsions is evidence of a pervasive and systemic bias.

Statistical data indicates that although Black students constituted 17 percent of the national enrollment, they received 37 percent of the corporal punishments, 32 percent of the out-of-school suspensions, and 31 percent of the expulsions (Office of Civil Rights 2001).

In the southern division of the Office of Civil Rights (2001), the issue of discipline is consistently identified as a problem by minority parents and groups. Stakeholders reported differential treatment of students resulting in racially disproportionate sanctions. The reported result of these actions has been the removal of a significant number of minority students from the regular school environment, the denial of equal educational opportunities, a higher school dropout rate, and the consequent deprivation of educational services.

NOT A NEW PROBLEM

Racial disparities in discipline referrals and sanctions are not a new problem but one that has largely been ignored by many school districts. Although many districts have become alarmed over rising discipline rates, they have not used disaggregated data to determine if the results were skewed (that is, if one group of students was overly represented), or if they did use disaggregated data and saw unusually high numbers of Black students, they assumed these results were to be expected.

More than twenty-five years ago, Office of Civil Rights data (1974) indicated that Black students were disproportionately subjected to disciplinary measures and were kept out of school as a disciplinary measure more frequently and for longer periods than nonminority students. At that time, it was also found that the "burden of fitting in" in desegregated schools was placed largely on Black students. Also, it has been reported that newly desegregated districts suspended and expelled disproportionate numbers of Black students and started them on a cycle that resulted ultimately in their dropping out of school (Eyler et al. 1983).

The Children's Defense Fund (1974) reported that minority students were suspended at younger ages than Whites, and that Black students were two to five times more likely to be suspended than White students in all regions of the country, received lengthier suspensions, and were more likely to be repeatedly suspended. Eyler et al. (1983) found that Black students were more likely to be suspended for "subjective" or "discretionary" offenses. Subjective offenses are those requiring a personal judgment and include disobedience, insubordination, disruptive or disrespectful behavior, profanity, and dress code violations.

THE PRICE OF DISCRIMINATION IN DISCIPLINE

For over twenty-five years, we have had a major equity problem related to discipline in our schools. By now, at least a generation of children, like the young man that I encountered, has cried out—but we as educators have failed to hear them. Instead of looking at ourselves and the school environment, we have concluded that single-parent homes, the lack of role models, television, and rap music are the sole reasons for the enormous discipline problems that we face in our schools today.

When students perceive inconsistencies in rules, detect favoritism, or feel disrespected and ostracized, they become angry, lose respect for us as adults, create ways to protect themselves emotionally, strike back, and become alienated from the learning process. Meirer et al. (1989) suggests that any type of discrimination, be it in academic grouping or disciplinary procedures, has predictable results: students become disillusioned and drop out or are pushed out (in the case of suspensions and expulsions), or do graduate but do not receive the same quality of education as other students receive. Beliefs, assumptions, and practices that result in racial disparities in discipline ultimately deny children the right and access to a quality education.

RECOMMENDATIONS

Step #1: Acknowledge the implications of over twenty-five years of data related to disparity in discipline.

Do: Start collecting disaggregated data pertaining to the race and gender of the referred students as well as the race and gender of the referring teacher. Collect data as to the types and severity of offenses by race and gender. This data is currently being collected by schools and the Office of Civil Rights.

CHAPTER 2

Merely a Symptom

What accounts for the disproportionate number of African American students who are referred for disciplinary action? I usually ask this question at the beginning of my workshop on discipline. Generally, I get a rush of hands; responses range from "no discipline at home," "single parent homes," "teenage mothers," "no Black role models," to "television" and "rap music." I agree with my participants that all of these can be contributing factors and I pose another question: What factors external to the student and his parents or factors inherent in the school environment contribute to the high rates of disciplinary referrals and actions involving African American students? To this question, there is usually no immediate response. After some probing, some brave teacher will usually say "sometimes it's us, our attitudes." With that statement, we can begin the process of addressing the disparity issue.

Disparity in discipline, as indicated by the most recent research findings, is only a symptom of a far more pernicious problem. The focus of this book is on the factors that extend beyond the student, his or her parents, and the family background; it is rather on those factors that are prevalent in the school environment itself that place a student at risk for disciplinary referral and sanctions, and perpetuate racial disparity in discipline.

School-related factors are those beliefs, attitudes, and behaviors that serve as catalysts for interpersonal misunderstandings and conflict, or that cause conflict situations to escalate. School-related factors may also include policies and procedures that leave room for bias. However, teacher and administrator beliefs and attitudes are most associated with disparities in discipline. Eyler et al. (1983) report that school climate and teacher attitudes are generally associated with disciplinary problems. Positive teacher attitudes about integration are associated with fewer disciplinary problems. It was also found that teachers who supported busing for desegregation perceived a smaller increase in disciplinary problems than teachers who opposed it. Racial disparities in discipline were associated with a lack of administrative support for integration and with school environments generally hostile to Black students.

Two school-related factors in particular contribute to disparities in discipline. The first factor is lack of knowledge, understanding, and sensitivity to the culture of African American students. The second school-related factor that negatively affects African American students, especially male students, is the set of faulty assumptions and negative expectations for the academic performance and social behavior of African American students.

Eyler et al. (1983) report that many teachers with socially heterogeneous populations are confronted with students whose behavior they do not understand, and they subsequently feel ill-equipped to respond or cope with the behavior. The styles of dress and behavior of some Black students may conflict with the teacher's values, resulting in suspensions and discipline problems. The lack of cultural understanding is most often a problem for non–African American teachers; however, African American teachers who are more assimilated into mainstream cultural values and beliefs may still experience problems relating to the cultural attributes and styles of their African American students.

Atkinson et al. (1983) describe a model of minority identity development where minority individuals ideally move from a "conformity" state to one of "self-actualization." African American teachers who are in the conformity state of minority identity development may: 1) identify more strongly with the dominant culture's values than those of African Americans, 2) lack awareness of their ethnic perspective, 3) exhibit negative attitudes toward themselves and other African Americans, and 4) accept and believe the prevalent stereotypes about African Americans.

In workshops, the difference in the social classes of some African American teachers and students has emerged as a factor that can be problematic in the teacher–student relationship. A lack of understanding of and sensitivity to the communication style of African American students can create tension between the teacher and student and lead to discipline problems. African Americans tend to be emotional and expressive when communicating. Their volume, tone, and nonverbal movements are often regarded as threatening to a teacher unfamiliar with this style of communicating. Teachers in some desegregated schools recognized that a lack of effective communication with students from cultures different from their own contributes to disciplinary problems (Eyler et al. 1983). Chapter 4 is devoted to the types of cross-cultural communication conflicts that can occur in the classroom.

The images, beliefs about, assumptions of, and expectations for African American students, especially male students, which are derived from historical stereotypes, contribute in a major way to racial disparities in discipline. The Joint Center for Political Studies (1989) reports that schools institutionalize social inequities through the gross stereotyping of Black children. Negative, inaccurate, and inflexible expectations formed by teachers, based on race and social class, result in the different treatment of minority and White students.

Racial disparities in discipline occur in a larger context in which cultural insensitivity and racial stereotyping combine to create a racially hostile and psychologically unsafe learning environment for African American students.

Hyman and Snook (1999) define *emotional maltreatment* as any disciplinary or motivational practice that psychologically hurts children. Practices that are considered to be psychological maltreatment in schools are humiliation and denigration; rejection, ignoring, and isolation; authoritarian discipline; sarcasm and put-downs; name calling; ridicule related to intellectual abilities; performance pressures; ridicule related to physical attributes and appearance; and bigotry (both conscious and unconscious) in the classroom. Daily, many African American students, especially males, enter classrooms in which they are misunderstood and stigmatized. Discipline referrals and sanctions that are the result of cultural insensitivity and unconscious stereotyping occur within school climates that can be considered to be hostile to African American students and, in effect, constitute psychological maltreatment.

One final note: the Office of Civil Rights (1994) considers an educational environment to be hostile when harassing conduct (for example, physical, verbal, graphic, or written) is sufficiently severe, pervasive, or persistent so as to interfere with or limit the ability of the student to participate in or benefit from the services, activities, or privileges provided by the district. The Office of Civil Rights also considers students to be the victims of different treatment if behaviors occur (based on the student's race or color) that interfere with or limit the student's ability to participate in or benefit from the services, activities, or privileges within the educational setting. In school environments where cultural insensitivity and unconscious stereotyping are allowed to persist and to influence disciplinary decisions, not only are African American students being psychologically maltreated, but their rights and opportunities to receive an education are being denied as well. Ultimately, racial disparity in discipline must be addressed as a moral, ethical, and legal issue.

RECOMMENDATIONS

Step #2: Acknowledge the magnitude and the pervasiveness of the problem.

Do: Design a climate survey related to discipline. Answer these questions:
   1. Are African American students, especially males, the victims of psychological maltreatment?
   2. Are African American students, especially males, being denied an equal opportunity to participate in the learning process through disparate disciplinary practices?

PART 2

CHAPTER 3

The Impact of Culture

Culture is a group's knowledge and expectations about appropriate modes of interaction and the patterns of activities that are common to that group. The social interactions through which children develop competencies reflect cultural values and standards for appropriate behavior. According to Greenfield et al. (1996), children come to school acting in accordance with the invisible cultures of their homes and communities, but conflict often arises when their behavior differs from the invisible culture of the school. In such situations, three things may occur: the school may devalue and even punish children for behavior their parents value; teachers may structure classroom interaction patterns that violate the invisible cultural norms of various minority groups; and such conflicts may not be recognized as cultural because of their invisible nature.

One of the sources of excessive disciplinary referrals is the lack of knowledge of and sensitivity to the culture of African American students. This cultural insensitivity is one of the major complaints I have received from African American parents in the Southern districts in which I work. Comments such as "they are insensitive to African American children" or "they don't know how to work with African American children" are often heard from African American parents. This insensitivity leads to misinterpretation of and faulty assumptions about the behavior of African American students. According to Butler (1992), an appreciation of African American cultural elements is a prerequisite to understanding and interpreting the behavioral patterns of African Americans. In order to decrease disciplinary referrals that result from cultural misunderstandings, teachers and administrators must understand the impact of culture upon the behavior of students.

MYTHS IN RACIAL STEREOTYPING

Although most educators would generally accept the notion that culture influences human behavior, the unique history and status of African Americans in this country poses additional problems to be overcome. A major barrier to understanding and appreciating African American culture are two myths that permeate American popular culture. Both myths, which have existed since Africans were enslaved on these shores, were created and perpetuated to rationalize and justify the enslavement of Africans. These myths are so deeply embedded in the American mind that the author has experienced workshops in which educators are resistant to even discussing the concept of an African American culture, or question its validity or functionality.

Myth #1: African Americans Do Not Have a Culture.

Many Americans, even educators, erroneously believe that African Americans arrived from Africa without the benefit of a culture, or that the culture of the enslaved Africans was totally eradicated during the voyage to North America and the process to make Africans accept enslavement. Beyond that, many people feel that African Americans as a group are simply a poor imitation of Euro-Americans. Although noted anthropologists such as Melville J. Herskovits (1958) have presented cognitive data supporting this fact, the resistance exhibited by many educators when this issue is being discussed indicates that the concept continues to be rejected at an emotional level.

Fact: African Americans Are a Historically and Culturally Distinct Group.

Butler (1992) describes African Americans as "a culturally distinct group of people bound by an ideological unity and a functional system of values and beliefs." According to Butler, "despite enslavement, psychological disorientation, social, cultural, and environmental displacement, old cultural patterns have persisted, some have been reinterpreted, others have been syncretized and adapted to fit the environment." Pinderhughes (1979), cited in Ho (1987), states that the cultural values of African American families are influenced by three major sources: 1) residuals from Africa, 2) identification with mainstream America, and 3) adaptations and responses to minority status.

Myth #2: African Americans Have an Inferior Culture.

The second myth acknowledges that African Americans have a distinct culture but that the culture is deficient in some way. The terms *culturally deprived* and *culturally disadvantaged* that were in vogue some years ago alluded to African Americans either being deprived of the traits of the superior Euro-American culture or terribly flawed as a result of having the deficient traits of African American culture. I felt I came from a rich culture in my small Southern fishing village and was shocked to find that the educational world I was entering as a professional teacher considered me to be culturally deprived. When I conduct workshops and explore the reasons for the behavioral problems that African American students experience, the response given is often "the poor values [cultural] that the students have learned."

Fact: African American Culture Is Different.

African American culture (like that of any other culture) is *different* from mainstream Euro-American culture but *not* deficient. First of all, it is a faulty notion to regard one culture as superior to another, as all cultures have norms and practices that meet the needs of the particular group. Secondly, all distinct groups, African Americans included, respond in certain, specific cultural ways.

Butler (1992) describes the core elements that establish the African American's identity and differentiate it from other groups as 1) self-identity, 2) knowledge, 3) emotion, and 4) behavior. Butler suggests that African Americans have distinctive ways of defining who they are and how they acquire knowledge, respond emotionally, and behave. According to Locke (1992), a number of distinctive characteristics of African American cultural traits give strong credibility to the uniqueness of an African American culture. Locke describes these elements as those 1) not found in the dominant culture; 2) connected in some way to the traits of other Afrocentric communities, i.e., Caribbean; and (3) those similar to the elements found in West Africa, the location from which most slaves came. Some distinct differences that Locke found between Western and Afrocentric cultures are differences in the concept of time (relative vs. linear) and the usage of the "be" verb (as illustrated in Black English) to emphasize whether something is done only at the present moment ("She bad") or habitually ("She be bad"). Locke asserts that the society may be that of the United States, but the values are African American, and that African American values come only through an African American culture.

Herskovits (1958) identified a number of cultural elements that are carryovers from Africa and that have survived in the United States. Some of these Africanisms are reflected in the behaviors of today's African American students. These cultural elements are:

- funerals
- magical practices
- folklore
- dance
- song
- motor habits (walking, speaking, laughing, sitting, postures, burden-carrying, hoeing, and movements made in various agricultural and industrial activities)
- ways of dressing hair (wrapping, braiding, cornrowing)
- wearing of head kerchiefs and scarves
- etiquette (the use of titles of respect, respect for the elderly, the practice of turning the head when laughing, placing the hand over the mouth, and averting the eyes or turning the face when speaking to respected persons)
- concept of time (approximations rather than punctuality; CP time; "colored people's time"—habitually arriving late—is culturally expected and accepted)
- cooperation and sharing (orientation towards collective responsibility and interdependence)

- child-rearing practices (the use of corporal punishment)
- adoption of children (informal)
- myths about abnormal births
- child-naming practices
- audience and performer styles (call and response)
- religious and spiritual expressive styles (highly emotional)
- conception of the devil

Hillard (1976), cited in Hale-Benson (1986), describes the core of African American cultural style. African Americans tend to:

- respond to things in terms of the whole picture rather than its parts
- prefer inferential reasoning to deductive or inductive reasoning
- approximate space, numbers, and time rather than stick to accuracy
- prefer to focus on people and their activities rather than on things
- have a keen sense of justice and are quick to analyze and perceive injustice
- lean toward altruism, a concern for fellow human beings
- prefer novelty, freedom, and personal distinctiveness (this is shown in the development of improvisations in music and in clothing)
- not be "word" dependent; African Americans tend to be proficient in nonverbal communication

Lynch and Hanson (1992) contrasted the beliefs, values, and practices of African American and mainstream culture. They found that African American culture is characterized by: 1) collective orientation, 2) kinship and extended family bonds, 3) high-context communication, 4) religious and spiritual orientation, 5) more authoritarian childrearing practices, 6) greater respect for elderly and their role in the family, and 7) more oriented to situation than time.

CULTURAL CONFLICTS IN THE CLASSROOM

Even if the African American student is acknowledged as having a culture, and one that is simply different, not defective, he faces yet another challenge. As Greenfield et al. (1996) suggest, the customary modes of activity and interaction (of minority students) often differ from those favored by the mainstream Euro-American culture in public schools. Although African Americas are not a monolithic ethnic group, with all members being attached to traditional cultural norms to the same degree, it can be safely stated that African American students generally must give up significant aspects of their cultural identity in order to be successful in the American public school system. Independence and individual achievement, aspects of the core mainstream value of individualism, with Anglo-Saxon and European immigrant origins, is highlighted in the cultural–institutional setting of American schools. Greenfield et al. (1996) suggest that this contrasts with the collectivistic cultural value orientation (which emphasizes interdependence) of many non-Western immigrants and minority groups, that is, Asian Americans, Hispanics, African Americans, and Native Americans. According to Greenfield et al., children from individualistic and collectivistic value orientations become adept at different modes of activity and have different conceptions of appropriate behavior.

Based upon the author's discussions with teachers and students, there are some cultural patterns that are especially problematic for African American students in the school setting. The behavioral aspects associated with the collectivistic value orientation of African Americans (for example, grouping behavior, the "we," social and cooperative orientations when misunderstood) can be precipitating factors for disciplinary actions involving African American students.

The grouping behavior of African American students can be very threatening and intimidating to some teachers in the school setting. The communalism value is held and practiced very strongly by African American students, especially in situations where they might be in a numerical minority population. It is very important to bond, to stick together, and even to protect each other if necessary. Sitting together in the cafeteria, at sporting events, and even walking together down the hallways is very important to African American students. This grouping, plus the emotional nature of African American communication (perceived to be loud), often calls attention to African American students. The problem occurs when African American students feel that they are unduly being singled out or harassed when they see other groups engaging in the same behavior.

The "we" orientation is also exhibited in conflict situations. When African American males hear about or see what they believe to be mistreatment or harassment of another African American, especially by an outsider, they assume a protective stance, which often leads to fights. Not only do African American males feel the obligation to protect other African Americans from students from other groups but from teachers as well, if necessary. African American male students often get into trouble by coming to the defense of another student when they feel the teacher is mistreating or picking on that student. In this situation, the responsibility to the group transcends the individual consequences that may result from this action.

The social orientation of African American students tends to make them appear more interested in socializing than in doing schoolwork. African American students are often written up for wasting time, not completing work, and excessive talking.

This social orientation is most important, however, in the teacher–student relationship. African American students have a high need to connect with the teacher, and to feel that the teacher accepts, respects, and cares about them as an individual. African American students are intuitively aware of the teacher's genuineness and caring. The quality of the teacher–student relationship will determine the extent to which discipline problems will occur with African American students.

The cooperative spirit of African American students is often misinterpreted as cheating. African American students distinguish between actual cheating and helping a friend find the page or "assisting" another student who is having a problem.

Other values related to culturally influenced personality traits could also be precipitating factors for conflict in the classroom.

The value of expressive individuality, which is interpreted as style and demonstrated in the fads in clothing, hairstyles, and mannerisms, can cause major problems for African American students. African American males in particular are found to express their individuality in ways that are unacceptable in the school setting. The wearing of too large pants, not wearing belts, and the showing of underwear are all unacceptable in the school setting. The wearing of sunglasses and hats indoors, which is inappropriate according to mainstream and school etiquette, is considered totally acceptable by many African American males. Sometimes, a style of wearing clothing, such as one pant leg up or males wearing cornrows, is incorrectly attributed to gang affiliation. A major cause of conflict between African American students and the administration occurs when students feel they are falsely labeled as gang members.

The concept of social time causes problems for African American students, many of whom are chronically tardy to school or to class. Many African American students move along very slowly when getting to school and to class; the social situation is much more important than the time schedule.

The need for spontaneity and flexibility causes problems, especially for younger African American males, who have difficulty sitting still and attending to one activity for long periods of time. Many young African American males are considered hyperactive and are often referred for special education placement because of their need for activity.

The rigid use of time is a mainstream (European) American value. According to Althen (1988), Americans regard time as a resource, that is, "time is money." The ideal person in this society, in a cultural sense, is one who is punctual and considerate of other people's time. Althen (1988) concedes that this attitude toward time is not necessarily shared by non-Europeans, who regard time as something around them rather than something to use. He states that one of the most difficult adjustments that many foreign businessmen and students must make in the United States is the notion that time must be saved whenever possible and "used" wisely every day.

The African American relationship to and concept of time has been problematic for them in this country since the enslavement period. According to Sobel (1987), "the use of time was at the heart of owners' criticism of slaves: they wanted slaves to change their perception of time and work." Time continues to cause problems for African American students. The concept of social time adhered to by many African American students causes them to be chronically late to school or class. I have even experienced this in my own home with two children who were gifted honor students, but who were consistently late because they could not adhere to a rigid time schedule.

It is important, however, for the teacher to distinguish between two groups of tardy students. "Adjustors" (who are adjusting time to fit their social definition) move along slowly, chatting with each other, and enjoying the moment when going to school or class. They are caught up in the moment and regard the social situation as more important than the schedule. With "avoiders," on the other hand, the focus of being late is to avoid unpleasantness, either because they are unable to perform adequately, or because they expect to have conflict with the teacher.

DEALING WITH TIME ISSUES

1. Realize that the concept of time enforced at school is only one group's way of relating to time. Like other aspects of deep culture, the way one relates to time influences one's view of the world and how to operate in it.
2. Have a dialogue with students about the ways different cultures regard time. Point out that the school culture requires that all students adhere to a rigid time schedule. Explain why punctuality is necessary in the school setting.
3. Allow students to brainstorm ways to incorporate flexibility in the classroom time schedule.
4. Talk to chronically late students; find out why they are late and determine if they are adjustors or avoiders. Use different strategies with each type of student; remember that being late to class is a symptom of a much larger problem for the avoider.
5. Be aware that some conflicts that occur in the classroom may be a rebellion against the rigid adherence to time.
6. Be as flexible as possible with schedules.
7. Give ample warning when changing from one activity to another.
8. Provide sufficient "wait time" for students to respond to questions (at least five seconds); African American males have a tendency to respond more slowly because they want to be absolutely sure of their response.

DEALING WITH ENERGETIC STUDENTS

1. Realize that it is quite normal for boys up to about ages seven or eight to be very energetic.

2. Distinguish between normal high energy and hyperactivity; hyperactivity includes a constellation of symptoms.
3. Release the concept of "controlling" children. Controlling children and teaching children are two very different concepts.
4. Focus on ways to fully engage students with high energy. Direct the energy into creative pursuits.
5. Rather than trying to control the energy, introduce new concepts to challenge the student. Many African American parents tell me that their "high-energy" sons are bored in the classroom.
6. Engage students in more "hands-on" activities.
7. Remember that the optimal attention span for an adult is only twenty minutes. Plan activities that allow for ebb and flow, short periods of intense concentration followed by a short break.
8. When high-energy children are grossly involved in an activity, be flexible with time; don't disturb them.
9. Praise high-energy students when they do follow directions.
10. Treat all students the way in which we treat gifted students; we "honor" their quirks.
11. Determine if birth order or other family issues are involved; is the child an only or the baby or the only girl or boy used to attention?
12. Recommend parenting skills, if warranted.

JUSTICE IN AFRICAN AMERICAN CULTURES

Another value that causes the most problems for African American students is that of the need for fairness, equality, and justice. African American students are keenly aware of unfairness; they are always vigilant, and analyze situations to determine if injustice has occurred. In this respect, African American males have a great need to be heard and to explain their side. Most often, conflicts occur and incidents escalate because the African American male student feels that he either 1) was not taken seriously, 2) was not listened to, or 3) was not given the opportunity to tell his side. When any of these three events occurs, the African American male will persist in talking to be heard or to state his case. Unless the teacher listens, this situation will build to a point where the student (in the words of African American male students) "snaps" or "goes off on the teacher." Many African American male students feel that this is the only way that they can get a teacher to really listen to them.

In a society in which many African American males feel a very fragile connection and future, their culture is all they have. Adolescent African American males attach very strongly to the values of communalism, expressive individuality, and justice. Their walk, their speech, their mannerisms, and their interactions will express these values. These values help to define their identity and to provide some level of stability in what otherwise might be perceived as a very precarious life situation.

HISPANIC/LATINO STUDENTS

Although this book principally refers to African American students, Hispanic/Latino students face similar issues related to discipline and cultural differences. The concepts and strategies described here can be beneficial to administrators and teachers who work with Hispanic/Latino students. It is important that educators consider these issues for several reasons. First, demographic studies indicate that Hispanics/Latinos will account for 44 percent of the nation's population growth between 1995 and 2025. Already, there are more Hispanic/Latino than African American elementary school children, and in approximately ten years, this will be true for all ages (Hodgkinson 2000). Secondly, current data indicates that, like African American students, Hispanic/Latino students are suspended and expelled from public schools at higher rates than their White counterparts. New federal findings showed that Hispanic/Latino students accounted for 14 percent of the suspensions and 16 percent of the expulsions (Johnston 2000). According to the Advancement and Civil Rights Projects at Harvard University (2000), like African American students:

1. Zero tolerance policies are more likely to exist in predominately Latino school districts than in predominately White school districts.

2. Latino children are more likely to be referred for disciplinary action and to be disciplined than are White children.
3. Latino children are more likely to be disciplined for minor misconduct and receive punishments disproportionate to their conduct than are White students.
4. Latino children are more likely to be suspended for "discretionary" offenses than are their White counterparts.

Third, like African American students, Hispanic/Latino students may bring cultural beliefs, values, practices, and communication patterns that are different from the mainstream orientation advocated in our schools. Ho (1987) describes five common cultural values that significantly influence Hispanic/Latino life: familism, *personalismo*, hierarchy, spiritualism, and fatalism. The value of *personalismo* is described as that by which a Hispanic/Latino defines his self-worth in terms of those inner qualities that give him self-respect and earn him the respect of others. "He feels an inner dignity (*dignidad*) and expects others to show respect (*respecto*) for that *dignidad*." Closely related to the concept of *personalismo* is the quality of machismo or maleness. Machismo is that quality of personal magnetism that impresses or influences others; it is a style of personal daring by which one faces challenges, danger, and threats with calmness and self-possession. It would appear that these two values, in particular, *personalismo* and machismo, if not fully understood or misunderstood, could create tension and conflict between the teacher and especially the Hispanic/Latino male student who espouses these values.

Zuniga (1992) points out that Latino cultures value 1) a collective orientation, 2) interdependence, 3) a collective group identity, 4) cooperation, 5) saving face, 6) emphasis on interpersonal relations, and 7) a relaxed time orientation. These values are in direct contrast to the mainstream cultural values of an individual orientation, independence, individual identity, competition, being direct, emphasis on task orientation, and time sensitivity. This contrast in core cultural values is another area in which the lack of cultural understanding or the lack of appreciation of the cultural values could possibly lead to conflict in the classroom and subsequent discipline problems. Also, differences in the communication style of the Hispanic/Latino student and the mainstream teacher (for example, showing respect by looking down) can be problematic. Locke (1992) states that Mexican Americans engage in verbal play. They rely heavily on jokes, jocular talking, and in-group humor to relieve tension and stress. Like African American males, this type of verbal play may not be understood or appreciated and may present problems for Mexican American students.

Finally, it is important to acknowledge the differences between the different groups constituting "Hispanics." Hispanic Americans are also known as Chicanos, Latinos, Mexicans, Hispanos, Spanish-speaking Americans, Spanish Americans, and Spanish-surnamed Americans (Ho 1987). It is also important to recognize that the different groups of Hispanics may have entirely different school experiences based upon their status and value in American society. Some groups will have school experiences more like African American students than other groups. The school experiences of Hispanic/Latino students who are, in Ogbu's (1978) terms, members of immigrant or caste minorities will differ greatly. Immigrant minorities are those who have moved into the host society, America, more or less voluntarily. Caste minorities, on the other hand, are typically conquered groups, or those who did not come to this country voluntarily. In America, African Americans, Native Americans, Mexican Americans, and Puerto Ricans are considered by some to be caste minorities. Cubans and other South or Central American émigrés, though they may be political refugees, are considered voluntary immigrants and immigrant minorities. Mexican American and Puerto Rican students' school experiences will most closely mirror those of African American students.

Locke (1992) describes Mexican Americans as a group, shut off from the usual avenues of achievement by prejudice and discrimination. Like African Americans, they are plagued by damaging stereotypes (for example, Mexicans are lazy, passive, and failure oriented). Although Puerto Ricans are the only immigrants who come to the mainland of the United States as citizens of this country, they are an extremely devalued group (Locke 1992). Younger Puerto Ricans who have grown up in low-income urban communities face the most problems. Like Mexican Americans, they are portrayed in a negative manner by the media. They lack a strong sense of cultural identity, and suffer from racial ambiguity that results in conflict between them and the dominant culture.

Like African American students, Mexican American and Puerto Rican students attend schools that are microcosms of the larger society. Mexican American and Puerto Rican students in particular may be more vulnerable to factors in the school environment, such as the lack of cultural understanding and stereotyping that contribute to their disproportional representation in discipline statistics. The same approaches described in this book to eliminate racial disparities in discipline, as they pertain to African American students, can be adapted for use in schools with predominately Hispanic/Latino populations.

TEN WAYS TO DECREASE CONFLICTS RELATED TO CULTURAL DIFFERENCES IN THE CLASSROOM

1. Realize that the denial and devaluation of the culture of African American students is *cultural racism* (see Lustig and Koester 1996).
2. Ask: "What works in a culturally diverse school environment so that the norms of all ethnic groups are to some extent acknowledged and respected?"
3. Facilitate dialogues on cultural attributes and identity so that students can distinguish between traditional positive cultural practices (collectivism) from negative cultural practices, for example, the wearing of pants with no belts (from the prison culture).
4. Facilitate dialogues that distinguish between stereotypes (which originate outside the group and are used to control the group) and cultural attributes (which come from the group itself and are used to meet the needs of the group).
5. Don't be quick to accuse students of cheating; you may be seeing an innocent display of cooperation.
6. Let students help determine classroom rules and school discipline codes.
7. Always leave room for negotiation.
8. Seek input from parents and individuals from the community regarding the issue of cultural differences and discipline.

9. Refrain from assuming that all the negative behaviors exhibited by African American students are aspects of traditional African American culture.
10. Incorporate some collectivistic values and practices in the classroom, for example, peer tutoring, cooperative learning activities, and whole-class teaching.

RECOMMENDATIONS

Step #3: Acknowledge the existence and value of African American culture. "Just acknowledging the existence of another culture validates it" (Greenfield et al. 1996).

Do: Reflect upon your beliefs about the culture of African American students. Use the resources listed in the bibliography to learn more about African American, Hispanic/Latino, and other cultures.

CHAPTER 4

Cross-Cultural Communication Conflicts in the Classroom

African American culture is an oral culture. Great significance is placed on the oral transmission of information. Traditionally, African beliefs, values, customs, and history were transmitted by word of mouth from generation to generation. In African American culture, great respect is afforded those who possess exceptional verbal skills. If one examines the leaders whom African Americans have chosen to listen to, they are, without exception, great orators.

The significance placed on oral skill in African American culture is so important that a major part of the socialization process, especially for African American males ages eight to fifteen, is the rite of passage associated with learning and using the language of the culture. According to Hale-Benson (1986), an important manhood rite for African American males is playing the dozens, an activity engaged in primarily by young men in which two opponents dual verbally. Derogatory comments are made about each other, and their respective family members, especially the mother. The successful player masters several competencies, including being able to think quickly, and to control his emotions.

This culturally approved and respected verbal skill causes special problems for African American males in the school setting. According to Dandy (1991), 1) African American males have historically been noted for talking a particular kind of stylized talk; 2) learning how to use this talk is an essential part of passage from boyhood to manhood; 3) teachers generally are unfamiliar with the rules, purpose, and intent of this stylized talk; and 4) often the students who are successful at using this talk are referred by teachers to remedial classes, special education classes, or classes for behavior disorders or the learning disabled. The manner and tone in which some African American male students, in particular, communicate is often considered to be disrespectful and even intimidating by some teachers.

CULTURALLY BASED COMMUNICATION PREFERENCES AND TABOOS

Each of the following communication preferences or taboos can create tension and cause conflict if not understood and respected.

Call and Response

This communication pattern is seen in African American churches when African Americans listen to speakers. It is permissible and expected that one respond verbally to a speaker; this usually indicates approval for what the speaker is saying and encourages the speaker to continue in the same vein. For instance, in church, it is permissible to say "Amen" or "say it" back to the preacher. When African Americans hear the speaker say something that they like, it is permissible to say "tell it like it is" or something similar to encourage the speaker. I always smile to myself when the "silence is golden" appears on the movie screen. It doesn't have the same impact for some African American moviegoers who customarily "talk back to the characters on the screen." One might hear "You tell him, girl!" or "Don't go in there!" to warn a character in the movie. Verbal disapproval is also allowed in some settings, for instance, at talent shows, where the audience indicates its disapproval through hoots, grunts, and the like.

This African American cultural form is foreign to and disapproved of in the school setting. The school rule is to sit quietly and listen to the speaker. Interrupting the speaker with encouraging as well as disapproving remarks is taboo. African American students who "forget where they are" and respond in this manner are considered to be rude and out of line. The student's response and feeling on the other hand, is "All I said was . . . " He then feels angry, and depending on the teacher's tone and type of response, he may continue to make remarks (out of order) to "get back" at the teacher for what he feels is "picking on him."

Distance

The relationship that one has with an African American determines how close one gets to him or her in a conversation. Individuals from outside the culture are usually not permitted to get as close unless a relationship exists with that person. In a conflict situation, it is appropriate to maintain a distance of at least three feet or arm's length. The comment "don't get in my face" indicates that one is violating an individual's space. Often, in order to show power and authority, a teacher will get into an African American male student's face. This is a major cultural taboo for African Americans; it is considered a challenge and will be treated as such. If the teacher does not respond to the student's warning to get out of his face, then the student will probably resort to some physical means to protect his "space."

Physical Contact

In the midst of a conflict, any movement touching the other individual is considered provocation. Two African American individuals may engage in a loud and very emotional argument, but may be nowhere near fighting unless one of them makes a provocative move. This move is usually an indication that one must protect oneself. When teachers touch or push or move students along, the student's response is usually "don't touch me." In some cases, the student will view the touching as provocation and respond in a physical manner. Again, as in the case of distance, a "relationship" will make the difference.

Eye Contact

Traditionally, African American children have been taught to lower the gaze to show respect and humility for parents and other adults. To stare at an adult is considered rude and is taboo. There are some African American parents today, however, who teach their children to hold their heads up and look every one in the eye as a means of maintaining their dignity. A problem arises when the teacher attempts to force an African American male to make eye contact when the student was taught to lower the gaze to show respect. Contrary to the belief of some teachers, an African American male's lowering of the eyes does not mean that he is lying or trying to hide something. It also is not an indication of low self-esteem in this instance. Many teachers who need to exert their power through attempting to force eye contact insist that they only do this because African American males must learn to establish eye contact in the job market. It is very important to separate the two; forcing a student to make eye contact in a conflict situation is not the same situation as a job interview, and can only lead to an escalation of the conflict.

Gestures

African Americans find the direct pointing of fingers to show authority, and finger-snapping to get one to move, to be inappropriate. When a teacher puts his or her finger in the face of an African American male, or snaps fingers to move him along, it is considered insulting, and the student will usually respond.

Emotional Expression

African Americans are "high-keyed" communicators, which means we are loud and emotional when talking about something that we are very interested in or have strong feelings about. When talking about something that is very important to us, we become very excited and animated. When we are engaging in a debate, we may express our opinions in a loud and emotional manner, even though we are not angry. Many times, outsiders to the African American culture may feel that we are venting anger or hostility when they hear us arguing a point. The loud and emotional manner in which African American males communicate is very threatening and intimidating to teachers who do not understand this communication style. Teachers will often send students to the office because they fear a fight is going to break out, when in actuality the students are only engaging in a verbal game of "sellin' wolf tickets" (loud, threats). When African American males and teachers are involved in a conflict situation, especially when the male feels he has been unjustly accused or has not been able to state his case, he may become louder and more animated. This is not an indication that he is ready to strike the teacher, only that he is trying harder "to be heard."

High-Context Communication

African Americans are known as high-context communicators. We are not "word-bound," and as such, derive as much meaning from what is not said verbally (the nonverbal cues) as from what is stated. African Americans watch the facial expressions, body movements, the stance, and even the changes in complexion when assessing a situation. African Americans place a high value on being genuine and "real," and use the nonverbal cues as indicators of genuineness. When an African American student says that a particular teacher does not like him or that a teacher is prejudiced, he is usually basing his beliefs on intuitive feelings and nonverbal cues. This, of course, often makes the African American student appear as though he is using "race as an excuse," because members of mainstream culture tend to utilize information obtained from words and the senses (rather than intuition) to make judgments.

Cultural Taboos

Asking personal questions, shaming in public, and the use of the terms "boy," "girl," and "you people" are highly offensive to African Americans of any age. African Americans have a concept of "my business," and are often suspicious when individuals appear to be too interested in their personal lives. "Boy," "girl," and "you people" are considered derogatory terms. Young African American males find "boy" to be particularly offensive and will ask a teacher whom she or he is talking to if addressed as "boy." Public shaming is a definite taboo; when an African American male is shamed in front of his classmates, he will take the shaming as a challenge as well as an insult, and will defend both his manhood and his dignity. Public shaming on the part of a teacher can only lead to a "lose–lose" situation. The student will invariably be punished for the outbreak that will occur after the incident, and the teacher will lose the trust and respect of the other students who observed the incident.

If teachers can become aware of and respect the cultural rules relating to communication styles, tension between teachers and African American male students will decrease; conflicts can be avoided and incidents will not escalate.

CULTURAL ETIQUETTE

The social forms to be observed in interactions with individuals from diverse cultural backgrounds are cultural etiquette. There are rules that govern all of our interactions with others, and rules for interacting with those who may come from backgrounds different from our own. What follows are some rules for interacting with African American males in the classroom, especially in conflict situations. When teachers follow these rules, they show a respect for the culture, the communication preferences, and taboos of African American students. These rules relate to each of the communication elements previously discussed.

Call and Response

Do explain that there are different types of responses that are appropriate for different kinds of activities. Allow students to establish rules for when a more culturally based style can be used—for example, when discussing current events or some political issue.

Distance

Do not get in his face. Maintain an acceptable distance (about an arm's length), especially when in the midst of a conflict.

Physical Contact

Do not touch him, especially in the middle of a conflict situation. If he needs to leave the room, give a friend permission to walk outside the room with him, and talk to him until he cools down (all with the student's permission, of course).

Eye Contact

Don't force him to establish eye contact. His not looking at you does not necessarily mean that he is lying, trying to hide something, or being defiant.

Gestures

Do not point your finger in his face or snap your fingers at him.

Emotional Expression

Do not assume that he is going to hit you or someone else if he is loud and animated. Most importantly, give him the opportunity to be heard, to defend himself, and to state his case. Doing this simple thing will decrease conflict with African American males to a significant extent. Also, learn to distinguish when he is strongly expressing an opinion or arguing the "principle of the thing" from when he is angry.

High-Context Communication

Listen to him when he says that he feels that you don't like him. Don't become defensive if he says that he feels you are prejudiced. Ask him what makes him feel this way. Do some self-reflection and determine how you feel about him and why.

Cultural Taboos

Never call him "boy." Most importantly, never shame him in public. Ask him to step aside or right outside the door to speak to him. Ask him if you two can spend some quality time talking about the issue later so that the problem can be resolved. Use the SSS method: the first "S" is "stroke," the second "S" is "sting," and the third "S" is "stroke" again.

First, say something positive about the student; next, indicate your disappointment in his behavior; then say something positive about the student again and your hopes for behavior that is more like the person that you know that he really is or can be. This technique can get a point across while defusing a situation; I have used it and it works!

If teachers will follow these communication guidelines, then classroom conflicts will decrease. After all, our goal is not to simply punish students, but to teach them more appropriate ways in which to behave and to prevent conflict and the escalation of incidents. When students get into trouble, they are not in class or in school; each day they are not in class or in school, their chances of success decrease.

RECOMMENDATIONS

Step #4: Follow the guidelines for cultural etiquette.

Do: Observe your feelings and behaviors when interacting with African American students, especially males. Determine what you can do to ease the tension between you and African American male students. Determine what you can do to prevent incidents from escalating.

CHAPTER 5

Stereotyping in the Classroom

I have spent the last ten years going in and out of classrooms and school districts in an effort to ensure that all students have access to the best possible educational opportunities and are treated fairly. Over these ten years, two things have become glaringly apparent to me: first, stereotypes are pervasive in the school environment; and second, the lives of students are affected in a major way as the result of stereotyping. Specifically, I have observed that

- Stereotypes shape the beliefs and behaviors of teachers and administrators.
- These stereotypes influence the relationships that students have with teachers and administrators, as well as the educational outcomes of students, especially as related to academic placement and discipline.
- These stereotypes most often operate at a programmed, unconscious level and generate an automatic response.
- The most pervasive, persistent, and negative stereotypes are attached to the African American male student.

Although the lack of knowledge and understanding of the culture of African American male students places them at risk for disciplinary actions, the problems that African American students, especially males, experience in the school setting are equally the result of faulty assumptions and erroneous beliefs based upon historical myths and stereotypes. These myths and stereotypes generate fear and the need to

exercise absolute control in the minds of many teachers, especially
non–African American female teachers, and create a vicious cycle from
which African American male students in particular cannot escape.

THE NATURE OF STEREOTYPES

Boskin (1970) states that a stereotype is a standardized mental picture
representing an oversimplified opinion or an uncritical judgment that is
tenacious in its hold over rational thinking. He further describes stereotypes as:

- being pervasive once implanted in the popular lore
- an integral part of the pattern of culture which operates within and
  at most levels of society
- affecting thoughts and actions at both conscious and unconscious
  levels
- operating at reactive levels of thought and action
- receiving power from repetition
- very powerful, "often so powerful that they can be dislodged only
  after a series of assaults on them"

These stereotypical images over time become part of the cultural
fabric of the society. They become central to the thinking and behavior of the mainstream society towards the targeted group. Most
significantly, the erroneous beliefs that result from these images are
generally accepted as truth, they are not questioned, and they remain
as part of the core belief structure of the larger society, unless
changed at an institutional level by the leadership, decree, or man-
date. By and large, anyone who grows up in the society is influenced
by these beliefs.

THE CULTURAL CONDITIONING PROCESS

According to Paul (1998) and Loewenberg (1970), we are culturally
conditioned to develop a set of erroneous beliefs based on stereotypes.
This is how the process occurs: as children, we are born "tabula rasa"

or "clean slate"; we learn what we are to believe about others from our environment. Then we receive messages from significant and powerful others that help us form our belief system. We receive messages from our parents, grandparents, aunts, and uncles—all the people whom we love and respect. When they tell us that a certain group of people is different from us, not as good as us, not to be trusted, or to be avoided, we usually believe them, because these are people that we trust, people who take care of us and meet our needs. We also receive many significant messages through the social learning context; everything does not have to be stated verbally. Non–African American children are taught to fear Blacks when they are told to check the security of their car doors when they see a group of African American males walking on the street. Anyone who grew up with the Aunt Jemima or Uncle Mose salt-and-pepper shakers learned a lesson, never stated verbally, about the subservient role of African Americans.

By the same token, if the individuals that we are told to respect and honor because they are heroes and leaders give us messages about certain groups through their speeches or writings, those messages also become part of our belief system. When Thomas Jefferson, the quintessential American hero, wrote of the inferiority of Blacks, his message became central to the belief system regarding the treatment of Blacks in this society.

These erroneous beliefs based upon stereotypes are transmitted from generation to generation. Unless the cycle is broken, by an individual or by decree, stereotypical beliefs are passed verbally and nonverbally from one generation to another. Unless corrected, children will hold the same beliefs as their parents and grandparents. Also, unless corrected, generations of students will develop beliefs from textbooks and history lessons based upon myths and stereotypes.

These erroneous beliefs become imprinted at a very early age. By age five or earlier, beliefs based on myths and stereotypes are already developed.

Eventually, these erroneous beliefs operate at a programmed unconscious level and generate an automatic response. In most instances, when we are reacting to an individual on the basis of a stereotype, we are unaware of it. This unconscious, programmed nature of stereotypes makes them so difficult to change.

Modifying erroneous beliefs will occur only through examining these beliefs at a conscious level, monitoring one's behavior, and practicing positive conscious beliefs.

STEREOTYPICAL IMAGES OF AFRICAN AMERICANS

Stereotypical images of African Americans have existed since the enslavement of African peoples in this country, and have become as American as apple pie. These images have played a major role in defining American culture and are a significant part of the American cultural belief system.

Rome (1998) states that the earlier belief of African slaves as inferior to Whites is very important to understanding stereotypes, because it shapes the ways in which African Americans are perceived today. He states further that it is important to understand the unique experience of African Americans in American history. No other group entered as slaves, and just as important, no other group has been victimized "across centuries" like African Americans because of the original enslaved status. Before I talk about these images further, I would like for you, the reader, to take an active role in this discussion. In the space provided in table 5-1 (or on a separate sheet of paper), I would like you to list the stereotypes that you have either heard of or are aware of that are attributed to African Americans, both male and female. List as many stereotypes as you can, but don't stop writing until you have a minimum of ten.

Table 5.1   List of Stereotypes

Stereotypes of African Americans
1.
2.
3.
4.
5.
6.
7.
8.
9.
10.

How did you feel as you completed this exercise? Acknowledging rather than denying the existence of stereotypes is the first step in their eradication. I have had many teachers become very uncomfortable when they are simply asked to list the stereotypes that they have "heard or of which they are aware." I often have to point out that I am not asking if they hold the stereotypes, but rather just to list them.

If you found this activity to be very uncomfortable, then I would say that you should give close attention to this and the following chapters.

Below are some of the stereotypes that are commonly attributed to African Americans. Which ones were on your list?

inferior	lazy	culturally deprived
irresponsible	musical have rhythm	on welfare
athletic	criminal	drug abusers
intellectually inferior	violent	dishonest
drug dealers	sexually endowed/ active	

Now look at another list of stereotypes of African Americans. Check off the ones that in some form or another are the same or are similar to the stereotypes that you listed.

the savage African	the unhappy non-White
the happy slave	the natural-born cook
the devoted servant	the natural-born musician
the corrupt politician	the perfect entertainer
the irresponsible	the superstitious churchgoer/citizen
the petty thief	the chicken and watermelon eater
the social delinquent	the razor and knife "toter"
the vicious criminal	the uninhibited expressionist
the sexual superman	the mental inferior
the superior athlete	

You probably listed or have at least heard some form of many of the stereotypes on this list. What is significant about this list is that it is entitled *The Nineteen Basic Stereotypes of Blacks in American Society* and was compiled by L. D. Reddick in *The Journal of Negro Education* in 1944. As you can see, stereotypes of African Americans are of a persistent and consistent nature.

THE CREATION OF THE STEREOTYPICAL BLACK

The discussion of racial stereotyping is an emotional, sensitive, and often uncomfortable topic. We are victims of a cultural conditioning process that we do not understand, nor do we know its origins. If we as educators are going to eliminate the deleterious effects of stereotyping in the classrooms, we must fully understand how and why stereotypes are created and perpetuated.

First of all, stereotypes are never innocent creations; they always serve a deliberate purpose. In the case of African Americans, stereotypes were created to justify the institution of slavery and to rationalize the contradiction inherent in its existence in an otherwise free society (Bireda 2000).

Oliver (1998) asserts that since Black people were brought to America in 1619 as slaves, derogatory words have been used to construct an American image of Black people as being innately lazy, ignorant, crime prone, promiscuous, and irresponsible. The linguistic stigmatization of Black people and the subsequent distortion of their image as a people have been used to rationalize discrimination toward them.

During various periods in American history, such as during the abolition of slavery in the North, after the Emancipation of slaves, during Reconstruction, and especially from the 1880s to the 1930s, negative images of Blacks influenced race relations by justifying discrimination and violence toward African Americans. At significant junctures in America's history, stereotypical images of African Americans have emerged to shape public attitudes toward them. The dominant caricatures of Blacks in American life are presented in table 5-2.

Stereotypical images of African Americans have historically been transmitted through five major sources: religion, history, social science, popular culture (ethnic notions), and the media. According to Newby (1965), in the three decades following the Spanish-American War, anti-Negro racism developed on two levels. The first consisted of systematic ideas developed by scientists, social scientists, historians, and religious leaders—groups who endeavored to create a racist ideology

Table 5.2   Dominant Caricatures of Blacks

Sociopolitical Period	Image	Purpose
Slavery	Mammy, Coon, Sambo, Tom, Picaninny	To justify slavery; soothe White consciences
Emancipation; Reconstruction World War II	Black Peril, Brute, lazy, dishonest, immoral	To justify violence; to eliminate economic competition
Civil Rights Movement; Black Power Movement, 1950s–1970s	menace, anti-White, aggressive	To discount and neutralize black activism
New Racism (subtle vs. open racism); Retreat from the issue of race, 1980s–2001	criminal, drug dealer, welfare queen, gang-banger	To halt black economic and social progress

supported by scientific, historical, and/or religious authority. At the second level, popular attitudes were formulated and expounded by journalists, politicians, and popularizers—groups who were concerned with molding or reflecting popular opinion. The images created by both groups were reflected in attitudes and policies, both national and sectional, toward African Americans.

For almost four hundred years, stereotypical images of African Americans have flourished in American society. Because of their tenacity and emotional appeal, stereotypes of African Americans have endured and have been reinforced in major societal institutions. Unfortunately, but understandably, our schools, as microcosms of society, harbor the same stereotypes of African Americans. The beliefs about and attitudes toward African Americans that are prevalent in the larger society exist in the school setting as well. Since stereotypical images of African Americans are part of the cultural psyche of America, and operate at a programmed unconscious level, administrators, and teachers (yes, even good teachers) may respond at an unconscious level to a stereotype. Becoming a teacher does not undo the years of cultural conditioning that all of us undergo.

THE MYTHICAL AFRICAN AMERICAN MALE

The most vicious, pervasive, and enduring stereotypes were attributed to African American males (Bireda 2000). Boskin (1986) describes two predominate images of African American men that were developed and flourished almost simultaneously for almost four hundred years: Sambo and the Brute. Both images were derived from the view of

African Americans as inferior (for religious, biological, anthropological, or historical reasons) and both images were originated by White Americans and were utilized as a means of maintaining their superior position in society.

Sambo was principally utilized to present a benign portrait of slavery. Sambo had two principal parts to his nature: he was both childish and comical. Above all, Sambo was very amenable to enslavement and to second-class citizenship. This image of the African American male was that of a natural slave-servant. He was nonviolent and humble. He most often played the role of buffoon, displaying outlandish gestures and physical gyrations. The Sambo image also portrayed the African American male as docile, irresponsible, unmanly, servile, grinning, happy-go-lucky, dependent, slow-witted, humorous, childlike, spiritual singing, and of course, watermelon-eating and chicken-stealing. Sambo was an image of the African American male that provided a measure of psychological safety and security. As long as African American males identified with the image of Sambo, they were considered to be non-threatening and were safe from harm to a certain extent.

The Sambo caricature, portrayed as the silly, stupid clown who was afraid of the dark, who was happy despite his condition, who was ever grateful for the paternalism of the enslaver, and who even defended slavery, was created during the early years of slavery and was intensified during the period when slavery was abolished in the North.

With Emancipation and Reconstruction came a new, more threatening image of the African American male: the *Brute* was born. African American males were portrayed as ignorant, corrupt legislators who stole government money, who pushed Whites off sidewalks, and as sexual predators who lusted after White women. The Brute was portrayed as being a primitive, animal-like creature noted for his sexual prowess, but unable to control his sexual impulses. In addition, the Brute, because of his violent nature, was thought to be prone to rioting and fighting. The image of the Brute created fear and the need to control the African American male.

The images of the athletic and rhythm-filled African American had their roots in the enslavement period as well. The role that the enslaved were required to fulfill next to that of being a laborer or a servant was that of the entertainer. Enslaved Africans were forced to dance on the slave ships (to exercise the enslaved) and on the auction blocks. On the plantation, dancing, singing, and playing musical instruments were encouraged, rewarded, and often demanded.

Athletics emerged as another aspect of entertainment (Boskin 1986). Enslaved men were often bet upon as they participated in sporting events such as bareback jockeys, boxers, wrestlers, and foot racers. Like the images of the dependent, irresponsible, corrupt, thieving, and violent African American male, the images of the superathlete and entertainer have endured for almost four hundred years as well. All of these images, as well as other images, were borne out of a particular historical context and were created to justify the status and treatment of African American males. Unfortunately, some variety of these same stereotypes survive today and continue to negatively affect young African American males in all aspects of society, from "driving while Black" to disparities in school discipline. When unconscious stereotyping of African American males occurs in the school setting, it produces faulty assumptions, false accusations, and fear of the African American male student. The resultant tension, misunderstandings, miscommunication, and conflict make it impossible for the African American male students and their teachers to develop rapport or workable relationships. Most often, African American male students become trapped in a cycle of alienation that spirals from disciplinary referrals to suspensions and expulsions to academic failure and dropping out (Bireda 2000).

RECOMMENDATIONS

Step #5: Accept the fact that even good teachers can be influenced by the unconscious effects of stereotypes.

Do: Monitor your thoughts and feelings about African American students, especially males.

CHAPTER 6

Cultural Conflicts, Cultural Conditioning, and Disciplinary Practices

The interaction of cultural misunderstanding and unconscious stereotypes affects the relationships between African American students and their teachers, and increases the risk that African American students will receive disciplinary referrals and sanctions. The lack of cultural understanding affects the discipline process in several ways.

First of all, misperceptions occur in two ways: what is interpreted as misbehavior (for example, heads lowered and eyes cast down in humility) is viewed as defiance; the behavior is judged solely on the basis of the teacher's own cultural standards (for example, the raising of the voice in an effort to persuade versus being an aggressive act). Secondly, projection may occur. In that case, since the teacher does not have accurate information on which to base behavioral interpretations, the only available information (that from culturally conditioned stereotypes) is used to make a judgment. Finally, inappropriate expectations, or lowered or extremely high expectations, can be held for the behavior of African American students.

When unconscious stereotyping occurs in the school setting, faulty assumptions, false accusations, and fear are commonplace. Miscommunication takes place, tension mounts, and conflicts between teachers and African American students result.

Stereotyping most often produces predictable results in the form of self-fulfilling prophecies, and always leads to tension and conflict in the classroom. First, in most instances, at an unconscious level, the teacher or administrator holds a stereotypical image and related erroneous belief about the African American student. Second, an event occurs in the classroom that elicits an automatic response from the teacher. Third, this response elicits an immediate reaction from the student. Fourth, the student's reaction confirms the belief held about the student and reinforces the stereotype.

The comments of one principal are an indication of the type of interactions that occur with African American students. When an African American male was given a referral, the principal remarked with obvious glee, "Ah ha! We've got him now." She had been annoyed for some time by what she considered his defiant attitude. The student was enraged by the principal's comment and proceeded to tell her so. The more the student vented, the more vindicated the principal felt. The student was now proving what she had always believed. The images and beliefs she held about him and African American males were confirmed; he was violent and out of control.

As was stated earlier, African American male students, in particular, are the victims of differential treatment that occurs because of stereotyping. They face similar experiences in school, as do older African American males in the larger society. If we fear African American males on the streets, we fear them in the hallways; if we follow African American males in stores because we believe they are thieves, then they become the "usual suspect" when something is missing in the classroom. Also, as in the larger society, when the African American male steps outside of his prescribed role, when the African American student asserts his manhood and defends his integrity, he is severely punished.

When teachers are more comfortable with the Sambo image of African American male students, they relate better to the jovial, playful African American male than the serious, quiet one who is perceived to have an "attitude." The Sambo image also creates greater acceptance for the African American male student who is submissive rather than assertive, the latter being perceived as aggressive or defiant (Bireda 2000). When teachers see the African American male as the Brute, they respond to him with fear; they are afraid to admonish him or to wake him when he sleeps in class. The Brute image leads to a preoccupation with control and unjust labeling. He is punished most often for minor offenses (Bireda 2000).

INEQUALITIES IN DISCIPLINARY PRACTICES

Inequities and disparities in disciplinary practices result from cultural misunderstandings and unconscious stereotyping due to cultural conditioning. Described below are ten consequences of cultural conflicts and stereotyping in the classroom.

Unrealistic Expectations

We tend to hold African American students to much higher standards of behavior than we do other groups of students. That is, we never allow African American males, in particular, the luxury of "being boys." They are routinely more harshly punished for misbehavior that is considered normal for youngsters. When young African Americans get off the bus, in many instances after long bus rides, they are expected (in the words of one African American teacher) "to walk like little soldiers" to the building. These unrealistic expectations begin in kindergarten when young males with high energy levels (similar to all young children this age) don't sit still and are assumed to be hyperactive. From the first day of school, the control of African American males begins. They are punished more often and more severely for the typical misbehavior of children.

Faulty Assumptions

On many occasions, teachers are very quick to assume that a misdeed is intended on the part of the African American male, when his actions are really quite innocent. The stereotype of the oversexed Black male looms just beneath the surface. The following two examples of this involve very young African American males. In one instance, a young male had been given a pair of 3-D glasses. He had spent the evening pretending to see through plants, walls, clothing, and the like. The next day he took the glasses to school (which he should not have been allowed to do). He told a Caucasian classmate, "I can see through your clothes." The teacher overheard the comment and referred the student to the office for "sexually inappropriate behavior." The parents were livid and explained that there was no sexual intent in his statement, he merely meant that his 3-D glasses could penetrate all types of surfaces, including clothing. In another case, a young African American boy went to the bathroom, forgot to zip his pants, and came out. One of his Caucasian female classmates told the teacher, who then referred the young boy to the office for "sexual harassment." His parents could not understand why the teacher could not have simply told their son to zip his pants. On occasion, Caucasian female teachers have spoken of African American males "exuding sexuality" or sensing a type of "sexual come-on" on the part of African American males, which produces a type of "sexual tension" between them and the student that they find uncomfortable.

Behavior Tracking

In the same way that African American students are tracked academically, they are tracked behaviorally. First of all, we expect him to misbehave, and when he does, he enters a track that he cannot escape. He will never start another day "tabula rasa"; he is tarnished. He will get no breaks and no second chances because once he misbehaves, he wears a label. I once observed in a classroom where the teacher pulled out a file that she keep on one African American male student in particular; she said that one of the first things she did each day was to date a sheet of paper and wait for him to misbehave because she knew he would. The result of behavior tracking comes in the words of an African American mother who was distressed because her son had dropped out of school. She begged him not too, but he said that he could not take it anymore because "they won't let me change."

Inconsistency

One of the complaints heard most often from African American males and their parents is that discipline is inconsistent; in their words, "there are different rules for different students." Many of the complaints of racism come from the student's perception that non–African American and middle-class students are not punished or are not punished as severely as are African American males. African American students are very much aware of any inconsistencies and are always watching to see if a teacher is going to be fair in administering consequences for misbehavior. African American parents tell me that they want their children punished when they misbehave, but that they want the same rules that apply for their children to apply to all others. In a workshop, a teacher told of how he had come to a level of greater awareness with regard to consistency in discipline. He had admonished two African American students for their behavior and said that the next person to make a sound is "out of here." Well, the next person to make a sound was a Caucasian male student who simply said "e." At that moment, the teacher said that he saw and felt the eyes of every African American student in that room; they were all waiting to see if he would be true to his word and send the Caucasian out of the classroom. He said that until that day, he never knew the extent to which African American students observed their teachers to see if they were consistent in applying the rules.

Leading Behaviors

In many cases, African American males are "set up" for misbehavior. The teacher knows which "button to push" so that the student "goes off" or becomes verbally abusive. I have been told by teachers that this is a technique that is often used by some teachers when they do not wish to have a student in their class on a particular day or any day. They simply say whatever they know will upset the student to the point that he reacts and is subsequently sent to the office. Lacking maturity, these students never seem to understand that this is a ploy. African American male students have complained to me, however, that often they "feel like they are in a constant battle."

Personal Disregard

Because African American students are expected to be lazy and irresponsible, to not care about their schoolwork or getting an education, in some ways, they become invisible. They often complain that they are ignored and not listened too. Most often, they complain of being disrespected. Many times, they feel that they are not listened too or respected until they "go off."

Failure to Take Advantage of Teachable Moments

Discipline involves both punishment and teaching. The focus of most disciplinary action with African American males is punishment. African American parents often ask why the school official didn't talk to their son and explain to him why what he did was wrong. An African American parent volunteer in the school bookstore observed the way in which two incidents involving the theft of a pencil from the bookstore were handled by a teacher. In the first instance, an African American male stole a pencil and was immediately referred to the office for ISS (in-school suspension). In the next instance, involving the same teacher, a Caucasian male stole a pencil. However, rather than being referred to the office, he was given a lecture on why it was wrong to steal. The volunteer felt that it was assumed that African Americans would steal and the little boy had to be "taught a lesson," while the stealing on the part of the non–African American student was considered to be a less serious matter.

There are other times when teaching is the most effective approach. An African American high school student referred to one of his favorite teachers as "his dog" and was overheard by an administrator. The administrator became very angry and admonished the student to never use that term again. The student was very confused and felt embarrassed and put down by the administrator. A much better way to have handled the situation would have been to make this a "teachable moment" and explain to the student that some terms, although appropriate to use when referring to and communicating with one's peers, are considered inappropriate in the school setting. In this way, the student would have learned a valuable lesson without undermining his self-esteem.

Failure to Acknowledge and Respect Cultural Differences

Stereotypes get in the way of acknowledging and respecting cultural differences. When one's beliefs about African American males are based upon negative stereotypical images, it is more difficult to view differences as differences rather than deficits. In these cases, the African American male will be viewed as loud and emotional because he is uncouth and untrained; his failure to establish direct eye contact will be a sure indicator of his dishonesty.

Excessive Punishment

A common complaint of African American parents is that the punishment often far exceeds the offense. There appears to be a belief that because of innate character deficits and a proclivity for thievery, fighting, and disruptive behavior, African American males who break the rules should be "made examples of," to warn all others that this behavior will not be tolerated. In one case, an elementary school student who was "clowning around" in the cafeteria was publicly paddled over the school intercom. In another instance following Halloween, a high school teacher allowed his class to eat candy in class. An African American male threw the stick from a lollipop out of the window. The student was told to do 100 push-ups and warned that if he stopped he would be made to start over. The student said that he would not do 100 push-ups because he physically could not do 100 push-ups (he was very slight in build). The student was referred for insubordination.

Intolerance for Nongroup Assigned Behaviors

The purpose of stereotyping is to control the targeted group, so stereotypes are always accompanied by a code or set of rules by which the victim of the stereotype must abide. These rules regulate the personal behavior of the targeted group. There has always been a written and unwritten code of behavior for African American males that, like the stereotypes themselves, has been transmitted from generation to generation. Like stereotypes, these codes operate at an unconscious level; without our awareness, they can influence our reactions to certain behaviors in African American males. When African American males violate this historical code, they are usually severely punished.

Below are five of the major historical or Black codes that governed the behavior of African American males, and the interpretation of the violations of these codes in the modern-day school setting.

Three or more Black males shall not gather.

It was originally felt that if Blacks were allowed to congregate, they might conspire against the enslavers. The sight of Black men gathering created fear in Whites. Today, the sight of three or more African American males still produces fear. Oftentimes, African American males walking down the hall or sitting together in the cafeteria can create feelings of uneasiness.

Never strike a White.

African Americans have always been severely punished for striking Whites. African American parents often complain that their son was punished more severely when he was involved in a fight with a White student. In many cases, the African American male is punished for starting a fight when he strikes a White student for using the "n" word. Most often, the White student remains unpunished for the use of the "n" word; what happens, in effect, is that the original victim of racial harassment and verbal assault now becomes the perpetrator of the offense.

Never raise your voice at a White.

When the African American male becomes emotional, his behavior is considered to be verbally aggressive or disruptive. In many cases, his volume increases when he is attempting to state his case or defend himself.

Never contradict a White.

When African American males feel that they are being treated unfairly, they will insist on "being heard." This behavior usually gets them into trouble and the student is labeled argumentative, insubordinate, or defiant.

Be submissive.

When African American males are not submissive in speech or manner, they risk the danger of getting into real difficulty. They are assumed to have an "attitude." This lack of submission is usually met with a show of power with the intention of showing them who is in control. Even

African American males who are excellent students get into trouble when they do not display humility or act "too proud." This "attitude" is what seems to be most offensive to many teachers and administrators. A middle-class African American teacher recalled how her two sons were treated very differently in the school setting. The oldest one, the smarter of the two, is also very serious. He doesn't joke or play around, and is considered to have an attitude by his teachers. His mother has often had to go to school to talk about his "discipline" problems. His younger brother, on the other hand, who is not as bright academically, is more outgoing and jovial. He is considered an ideal student and has never had a discipline problem. The mother of these two students is certain that it is her elder son's lack of submissiveness that is problematic for him.

The belief that the African American male must be controlled is based on the historical image of the Brute. The need to exercise control and to demonstrate authority is one of the major causes of tension, conflict, and disciplinary problems involving the African American male student. When a "show of power" is used unnecessarily, it will provoke a negative reaction in the African American male student. He will most definitely strike back when he feels that he is challenged, humiliated, ignored, or treated unfairly. This, of course, creates a lose–lose situation in the classroom. The African American male student will most definitely lose because he will face some type of disciplinary action. The teacher also loses, however, because students are always watching, and they will lose respect for the teacher who must exercise power in this manner.

African American students, in epidemic proportions, are being trapped in a cycle that leads to disciplinary referrals, detention, in-school suspension, expulsion, or placement in an alternative setting. This cycle ultimately ends with academic failure and dropping out. For many, the future beckons even more bleak: incarceration is the last stop in the cycle.

RECOMMENDATIONS

Step #6:   When you write a referral, ask yourself if the offense or conflict is in any way the result of misperceptions, the projection of stereotypes, or the result of inappropriate expectations.

Do: Dialogue with students about your interactions and relationships with them.

PART 3

CHAPTER 7

Changing The School Climate: The Administrator's Role

Eliminating school-related factors that place African American students at greater risk for disciplinary referrals and actions requires that fundamental and significant changes occur in the school culture and environment. Two types of changes on two different levels must take place. Changes related to *culturally responsive* and *culturally responsible* actions must occur at both the institutional and individual levels.

Culturally responsive actions include those social practices that acknowledge and respect cultural differences, especially those differences that occur in communication patterns and styles. This change is based upon the recognition that a student's identity is shaped by his culture and that *cultural connectivity* is essential for his healthy functioning and growth. To require an African American student to deny his culture is to require him to deny a core part of himself. From my many years of experience as a codependency counselor, I know that the denial of the self is very destructive to the individual; this type of denial produces a marginalized rather than a healthy individual. Also, it is important to remember that the ultimate attempt to control or dehumanize enslaved African people was to try to destroy their cultural identity and deny them cultural expression. We do not want to repeat this type of culturally destructive behavior in our school settings.

Respecting the African American student's cultural identity does not mean that we don't have rules and regulations. It does mean, however, that we recognize that in a diverse society, in schools with culturally diverse student populations, the policies and regulations that we establish must neither give privilege to any particular group nor penalize any group because of cultural differences. At the institutional or school level, changes that relate to cultural responsiveness involve a revision of policies and procedures that are discriminatory and leave room for abuse. It also includes a system of teacher accountability and evaluation that emphasizes the teacher's ability to demonstrate culturally sensitive and responsive behaviors toward all students. At the individual level, cultural responsiveness involves honestly assessing one's beliefs about African American students, and one's interactions with them. It also involves the practice of *cultural etiquette*. To create a school environment in which culturally responsive and culturally responsible behavior is the norm requires courageous leadership on the part of the principal, and a commitment to the process by the faculty and staff. In this chapter, I discuss the principal's role in changing the school climate, and the process that must be undertaken if a school is serious about reducing the disciplinary problems encountered by African American students.

THE PRINCIPAL'S ROLE

From my work in schools, I have come to believe that the principal's attitude and commitment to creating a culturally sensitive school environment is the most important element in bringing about the needed changes. The principal must set the tone, initiate the process, guide the process, and hold teachers accountable for creating a classroom environment in which all students feel respected and treated fairly. The role of the principal is to provide the leadership necessary to create a school environment that is characterized by both culturally responsive and culturally responsible behaviors toward students. Ultimately, the principal has the responsibility for ensuring the elimination of any school-related factors that place African American students at risk for disciplinary referrals.

In order to create this culturally sensitive school environment, the principal must give attention to the outcomes of specific groups of students, especially those students who are most at risk of experiencing difficulties in the school setting and becoming noncompleters—generally, poor African American males. The principal must model culturally responsive and responsible behaviors, provide needed information to increase teacher competency, and coach those teachers who are uncomfortable or resistant to the process. Finally, the principal must set the standards for professional ethics and establish the criteria for evaluation as it pertains to cultural sensitivity in the specific school environment.

The principal must provide leadership in three key areas: 1) initiating the process, 2) guiding the process, and 3) evaluating the process. In this chapter, I provide strategies for initiating and guiding the process. In chapter 10, I discuss evaluating the effectiveness of the process in creating a school environment that is sensitive and responsive to the culture and experiences of African American students.

INITIATING THE CHANGE PROCESS

In the initiation phase of the process, the principal must determine the faculty's

- attitudes toward African American students
- perceptions of the need to specifically address issues related to African American male students
- openness to participate in the process
- level of support that is needed to make the process successful
- sense of buy-in or ownership of the process

Step 1: Assessing Faculty Attitudes toward African American Students

The attitudes held by faculty members towards African American students will, to a large extent, determine the faculty's perception of the need to examine school-related factors that may lead to disparities in the disciplinary process. The first task of the principal, therefore, is to make some determination about the attitudes held toward African American students. This can be done in two ways: by conducting an informal climate audit and through dialogues with faculty members. Since beliefs precede behaviors, the best way to get a feel for teacher attitudes toward African American students is to observe interactions between teachers and students in classrooms and other campus settings. The purpose of the observations and the dialogues is to help the principal determine the beliefs that are held about, and the feelings toward, African American students. At this point, the principal should also be interested in determining the extent to which faculty members understand or feel that they understand the culture of African American students. Finally, it is important to see the type and quality of interactions between African American students and their teachers. A point of departure for the dialogues may simply be "We seem to be experiencing a number of disciplinary problems with our African American male students. What do you feel is the cause of these problems?" It is important at this point for the principal to create a climate in which faculty members feel free to express their beliefs and feelings toward the students. To eliminate the school-related at-risk factors for African American students, changes will have to occur in the faculty's 1) belief system regarding African American, 2) feelings toward African Americans, 3) level of knowledge about the culture of African Americans, and 4) interactions with and behaviors toward African American students.

Step 2: Establishing the Need for Change

As I was in the process of completing this book, I received a call from an administrator who was interested in my working with her faculty on issues related to African American males. Like many schools, they had a disproportionate number of African American males who were referred for and were the recipients of disciplinary actions.

The principal was concerned, however, about resistance from the faculty. It seemed that several faculty members were complaining that the focus of the training was on African American males. It was their feeling that they should be concerned about all of the students rather than focusing on this group of students. In this case, the principal would have to establish or indicate the need to focus on this particular group of students. To help establish a need, today's principal has to rely on statistical data, disaggregated by race, gender, and social class, if possible. By using this type of data, a picture will emerge that clearly shows the group of students that presents the most critical need for attention. Given that all faculties are interested in preventing and decreasing the number of discipline problems rather than merely punishing the students who commit offenses, the principal must determine the root causes of the problem.

Conducting separate focus groups with teachers, students, and parents can provide insights that will support the need to focus on the issues related to African American students and discipline. At one parent forum that focused only on the issue of discipline, sixty-five African American parents attended. School officials were amazed because they had previously had little success in getting African American parents to attend meetings. The attendance of these parents decried the myth that African American parents do not care about their children's education. These parents were very concerned about what was happening to their children, and disparity in discipline was a major concern. Also, to the surprise of the school officials, these African American parents did want their children disciplined. They, however, wanted discipline to be administered in a fair and consistent manner. In one of the districts in which I work, the superintendent's attitude is that "If there is a perception of a problem, then there is a problem." African American parents are starting to voice many concerns, and to seek redress in the courts for issues related to disparities in discipline.

Although many faculty members may not be as inclined to hear the opinions of students regarding why they misbehave, and the disciplinary process in general, I do recommend that input be solicited from students as well. It is important to hear from the students who are experiencing the most problems in the area of discipline. It was after hearing the feelings of students, especially those who were frequently in trouble, that I decided to look into and address the school-related issues.

Step 3: Motivating the Faculty to
Be Open to the Process

In order to reduce disproportionality in disciplinary referrals and to eliminate school-related factors that contribute to the problem, the faculty must be willing to participate in the process. A combination of the "stick and carrot" approach appears to be the best approach.

The "carrot" in learning how to better understand and relate to African American students is that it will simply make life easier for the teacher. Cross-cultural interactions can be very stressful if one does not understand or appreciate cultural differences. Holding stereotypes, even unconscious ones, produces stress in the form of fear and the feeling that one has to constantly maintain some sense of control when interacting with the stereotyped individual. Adopting culturally responsive and responsible behaviors will reduce teacher stress, promote better relationships with African American students, and add to teaching effectiveness. From a basically selfish point of view, teaching African American students will become infinitely easier if the teacher actively engages in this process.

From the point of view of teacher accountability and professional standards, teachers have an ethical responsibility to learn how to effectively teach all students well. Teaching today is not like it was when I started teaching in the 1960s. Most of us teach students who come from cultural backgrounds very different from our own. Some of us teach students that we never thought we would teach, and unfortunately, through the process of cultural conditioning, may have negative views of and hold low expectations for those students. Teaching a diverse student population is the new reality; these are our customers, these are the students that we are ethically bound to teach in the best way that we can. Learning accurate information and unlearning erroneous beliefs is part of our responsibility as professional teachers; it is also the key to our professional empowerment. Once, in a workshop, as I talked about the new student population, the new challenges, and the new paradigms that we as teachers would have to adapt to, a teacher bemoaned this new teaching reality, and wondered out loud, "Why can't things just be the way they were fifty years ago?" Well, unfortunately or fortunately, things are not, and will never be, the way they were fifty years ago. The new teaching reality requires that teacher evaluations and promotions consider culturally responsive and responsible behavior as part of the evaluation criteria. The principal must in no uncertain terms make it clear that in this school environment, teacher effectiveness includes the willingness to grow as a teacher (actively participate in the change process) and the demonstration of culturally responsive and responsible behaviors.

Step 4: Support the Development of New Competencies

Professional development in the form of training related to African American culture, African American male identity issues, and dealing with stereotypes must be provided for the faculty. The lack of accurate information about African American culture and African American males is a major contributor to the problems that occur between African American male students and their teachers. This professional development should not be limited to a day or two of training, but should include the opportunity for teachers to engage in ongoing dialogue about the issues. Instituting a buddy system matching teachers who have problems with teachers who are most effective in teaching African American students and who have few discipline problems with these students can be very beneficial. There is always at least one teacher who can establish a relationship with the most troubled student. Have the teachers who are experiencing the most problems (the most referrals) seek advice from and observe the more effective teachers.

It is important for the principal to emphasize throughout the process that this is not intended as teacher bashing; it is a way to help teachers find ways to be more effective in reducing tension and conflict between themselves and African American students.

Step 5: Promoting Ownership of the Process

This process is intended to change the school culture. As such, it requires not only the active participation of the faculty, but also their "buy-in" and ownership of the process. Reducing disciplinary referrals and actions among African American male students must be a school goal. Eliminating the school-related factors that contribute to these disciplinary referrals and actions must also be a school goal. It is imperative that this process become a schoolwide project, with a plan developed to systematically bring about change. Although the principal has the responsibility for initiating and guiding the process, all members of the school community must be included in the process: teachers, students, parents, and interested community leaders.

ENSURING EQUITY THROUGH CHANGES IN POLICIES AND PROCEDURES

Eliminating school-related factors that lead to disparities in the disciplinary process require that changes occur at the policy-and-procedure level. This process will be initiated by the principal and implemented through the involvement of teachers, parents, students, and individuals from the community.

Below are suggested ways to make changes in policies and procedures that will promote culturally responsive and responsible behaviors related to the issue of discipline.

1. Form a committee made up of teachers, students, parents, and community members to review the current student disciplinary policies and procedures.
2. Make revisions in policies where necessary to ensure that there is no possibility for vague interpretations, abuse, or disparate treatment.
3. Clearly define the criteria for offense categories. What is considered disruptive, disrespectful, defiant, argumentative, or verbally aggressive behavior depends a great deal on subjective or individual interpretation. Try to come to some clear and consistent interpretation that leaves little room for unfairness.
4. Base assessment of punishment on objective criteria. Leave no room for excessive or retaliatory punishment.
5. Clearly define how disciplinary sanctions will be imposed for specific offenses.
6. Make the examination of precipitating factors or events a part of the disciplinary process. It is important to rule out any instance of harassing or provocative behavior on the part of the teacher.
7. Allow input from a number of individuals prior to the imposition of serious sanctions (long-term suspensions, expulsions, or placement in an alternative school setting).

8. Any deviations from the established student disciplinary policies and procedures must be documented and approved by the committee that reviewed student disciplinary policies.
9. Establish policies and disciplinary penalties for racial harassment if none are in place.
10. Implement a procedure for providing conflict resolution training for teachers, and establish criteria for the participation of the teacher and student in the conflict resolution process.
11. Establish a procedure for assisting teachers who make an excessive amount of referrals for offenses that could be handled in the classroom.
12. Establish a procedure for investigating allegations of racism, classism, and other abuses of power.

Two additional changes must occur if school-related risk factors are to be eliminated. First, the importance of establishing good teacher–student relationships must be emphasized. Students learn through their interactions with teachers. The quality of the teacher–student relationship will determine the effectiveness of that interaction. It is also important to remember that African American students are socialized in a collective culture. Social relationships are important and that includes the student's relationship with his teacher. When teachers have good relationships with African American students, discipline is less of a problem.

Second, the stated and unstated emphasis in the school setting must be on academics rather than discipline. There is a distinctive difference in the feel of schools whose focus is academics versus those schools whose focus is control and discipline. In many cases, schools with a predominately African American or low-income student population emphasize discipline rather than academics. For example, in schools that I have visited with a predominately minority and lower-income student population, I saw more information on bulletin boards relating to following the rules and building acceptable character. On the other hand, bulletin boards in the schools that emphasized academics were devoted to content areas of the curriculum and providing new information. For some reason, it appears at least from the informal curriculum in many schools that I visit, minority, especially poor African American students, spend more time in improving their character and learning to follow rules than focusing on academics. It is ironic, however, that in schools where the emphasis is on good teaching, with high expectations for student success, discipline tends to be less of an issue.

RECOMMENDATIONS

Step #7: Determine the changes that are necessary to make your school environment more culturally responsive and culturally responsible.

Do: Initiate the change process in your school.

CHAPTER 8

Changing Individual Attitudes

At the heart of the matter is a simple equation: balancing the relationship that exists between the African American student, his culture, and his teacher. The quality of that relationship will determine if communication and rapport, or tension and conflict, occurs between them. A lack of knowledge and understanding of the culture of African American students will interfere with the creation of effective communication between the teacher and student. Faulty assumptions, erroneous beliefs, and fear that result from historical stereotypes will block the development of a healthy relationship between teacher and student.

Changes in the school climate can only come about if changes occur at the individual level. The will to be more effective in establishing rapport, communicating, and developing relationships with African American students is essential.

Some years ago, I assisted a Superintendent's Advisory Committee in developing a Cultural Awareness Guide for all current and incoming teachers at one of the schools in which I worked. One of the major issues that the district was addressing was racial disparity in discipline. Tables 8-1 and 8-2 were developed by the Discipline and Classroom Management Writing Team. These exercises are for you, the reader. Reflect and answer the questions on the self-evaluation as honestly as possible. Don't be afraid of seeing areas in which you need to improve or develop; a conscious awareness of your relationship issues with African American students is key to correcting these issues and decreasing conflicts with African American students. The Do's and Don'ts presented in table 8-2 are excellent techniques for decreasing tension, conflicts, and discipline referrals.

Table 8.1   Self-Evaluation

Directions: Please read and answer honestly. No one will see this but you.

Question	Yes/No
1. Have you had an excessive number of discipline referrals in the past?	_____
2. Do you bring personal issues into the classroom?	_____
3. Do you tend to have excessive referrals on a particular student?	_____
4. Do you tend to demand eye contact from students?	_____
5. Do you have your classroom rules posted and stated clearly?	_____
6. Do you utilize the services of the school counselor?	_____
7. Do you utilize the suggestions of the school counselor once you have referred a student?	_____
8. Do you show your students respect?	_____
9. Is your classroom structured to ensure that students are actively engaged in learning?	_____
10. Do you encourage student interaction among diverse cultural groups (for example, seating arrangements and cooperative groups)?	_____
11. Do you set high expectations for ALL students?	_____
12. Do you discuss former students with other teachers in a negative way?	_____
13. Do you have any preconceived notions about a particular group of students?	_____
14. Do you hold grudges against students?	_____
15. Do you punish students excessively?	_____

Four broad categories of strategies are helpful to the teacher and administrator in developing attitudes and behaviors that will enhance the relationship between him or her and the African American student. First, acquiring accurate information about the cultural attributes of African American students, acknowledging and appreciating the differences between African American and European-based mainstream culture, and practicing the cultural etiquette described in chapter 4 are a starting point. Secondly, two instruments designed by the Superintendent's Advisory Committee can be very beneficial in assessing relationships with students, and in providing culturally effective classroom management strategies (see tables 8-1 and 8-2). Third, following two basic rules related to making referrals that stem from inappropriate student behavior can help you make the most effective type of referral to

Table 8.2 Culturally Effective/Ineffective Classroom Management Techniques

DO	DON'T
allow student to have time out after disciplinary action has been taken	have too many rules
allow students point of view to be heard	get in the face of a student (sign of aggression)
use "teachable moments"	yell
keep your "cool"	demand eye contact
post reasonable rules	touch (in a situation with anger)
refer problem students to counselor	demand student to use "Yes, Ma'am" or "Yes, Sir"
be willing to try counselor's strategies	call students "boy" or "girl"
be aware of your own baggage (for example, having a bad day or argument with spouse)	make situations a power struggle
	deny students their right to be heard
be consistant	take it personally
realize you are not perfect	expect submissiveness (threatening)
be willing to say you are sorry	allow/encourage hearsay (mutual
expect respect for authority	respect)

change student behavior. Finally, engage in a *cognitive restructuring process* to identify, challenge, and change erroneous beliefs based upon culturally conditioned myths and stereotypes.

WHAT, WHEN, AND WHERE TO REFER

"Seasoned" teachers have expressed with pride to me that they make few referrals to the office because "I can handle my problems myself in the classroom." One reason that "they take care of their own problems" is that they feel it is part of "good teaching." Secondly, they do not want to convey the message to the student that they are unable to handle them. Thirdly, they will say that they have learned from experience that whoever disciplines the student is the adult who earns the student's respect, and they refuse to give away their power. One aspect of good classroom management is learning what, when, and where to refer students when inappropriate behavior occurs in the classroom. Two guidelines that teachers with good classroom management follow are:

1. Remember that all human behavior is goal-directed; there is some need that the student who is acting out is trying to meet. Ask yourself: "Why is this student acting-out? Why is this student frustrated in this class?"

2. A referral should always assist the student in some way to change his or her behavior; therefore, even discipline should be more than simply punishment. In an educational setting, there must be an educational component as well. Ask yourself: "How will this referral help the student to change his or her behavior?"

Glasser (1986) posits that still another question be asked: "What can the teacher do to help the disruptive student to find the class more satisfying?" He suggests that only a discipline program that is also concerned with classroom satisfaction will work.

"Exceptional" teachers, counselors, and social workers who are also peer facilitators described student behaviors in terms of four categories of teacher responses: 1) incidents to ignore, 2) incidents in which the teacher would take advantage of a "teachable moment," 3) incidents that provided the teacher an opportunity to examine his classroom management style, and 4) incidents that required a referral of some type. The referrals were of six types: 1) counselor, 2) parent, 3) peer, 4) Student Support Team, 5) adult mentor, and 6) administrator.

The facilitators felt that some incidents did not warrant giving the student the power to draw attention away from teaching the class; if the behavior persisted, and was truly disruptive for the class, then it would be dealt with. They felt that teaching is part of disciplining, and that some incidents would not occur again or would lessen if students were taught why they were inappropriate. The teachers also felt that some number of incidents could be prevented if the teacher used more effective classroom management skills. As you will see in table 8-3, these "exceptional" and "seasoned" teachers referred only the most serious offenses to an administrator.

GIVING UP THE NEED TO CONTROL

The one thing that was central to the discipline practices of these teachers-facilitators was that they had no sense of a need to "control" their students. They believed that they should focus on "good teaching" — challenging, hands-on activities to keep students involved so that they didn't have time for excesses; cooperative learning and peer tutoring that allowed "structured socialization" so that students didn't feel constrained and deprived of peer contact; and most importantly, letting every student know that the teacher expected them to learn because the teacher had the ability to teach them.

The moment a teacher looks out at her class and feels that the only way she can teach is to get and keep them under control, she has lost the battle. The need to control always comes from a sense of fear—fear of our own inadequacies or fear of the students that we are assigned to teach. Most fear of the students we teach comes from culturally conditioned beliefs; for example, they are undisciplined, aggressive, violent, out of control, and prone to riot, etc. There tends to be a long-standing, deep-seated historical fear of African Americans, especially males, in groups, whether it be on street corners, in school hallways, or classrooms. We rarely fear White, upper-class males, even though this group of students has committed our greatest school tragedies.

Low expectations for behavior and fear are communicated nonverbally to students. They intuitively sense a teacher's fear and will test your resolve at every turn. They will also resent the fearful teacher because they are angered by the teacher's perception of them. The best rule to probably follow is to never teach a group of students that you fear. It is more productive for both you and the students if you teach those students with whom you are comfortable.

Dealing with fear issues and giving up the need to control African American students will be a great step toward decreasing tension in the classroom and improving relationships with African American students. This in no way implies that there should not be rules and expectations for appropriate behavior. It is ironic that the best teachers are also the "toughest," in the sense that they have rules that they expect students to follow, not to control them but to make the classroom run more efficiently. They do not fear students and they feel no need to control students. Most importantly, they refuse to give their power away. These teachers trust their students to meet the high expectations they hold for them, they are always teaching in social as well as classroom situations, and they trust their power to teach and make a difference in the lives of all students with whom they come in contact.

Table 8.3   What, When, and Where to Refer

Incidents to Ignore	*Incidents to Take Advantage of the Teachable Moment*
Habits (for example, sitting on legs, rocking in desk, chewing on pencil, shaking legs, tapping)	Name calling
	Student says "I can't do this"
Noisy hair beads	Ridiculing another child's clothing or work
Passing notes	Teasing other students
Shirttail out	Tattling
Pitching paper into trash	Using inappropriate nonprofanity (for example, "frigging, sucks, crap, freaking")
Chewing gum	
Tapping another student	
Nonverbal language: rolling eyes, popping lips	Talking or laughing when another student is talking
	Anger (count to ten)
	Not wanting to play together
Incidents to Examine Classroom Classroom Management Style	*Incidents Requiring a Referral*
Excessive talking	*To a counselor:*
Sleeping students	Bullying
Tardies	Stealing
Not bringing materials to class	Fighting
Requests to go to bathroom	
Students begin to converse after extended lecture (may need a break)	*To a parent:*
	Stealing
	Bad language
Sharpening pencil (inappropriate time)	Doesn't complete assignments
	Fighting
Getting out of/remaining in desk	
Name-calling	*To an adult mentor:*
Picking on others	Apathy (academics)
	Doesn't complete assignments
Incidents Requiring Referral to Student Support Team Administrator	*To a peer:*
Fighting	Apathy (academics)
Weapons	Behavior (better behaved student)
Threats	Academics (peer tutor)
Defiant behavior	
Sexual harassment	

COGNITIVE RESTRUCTURING PROCESS

As you read this section, it is important to remember that its intent is not teacher or administrator bashing; it is rather to enhance both personal and professional empowerment. Keep these three thoughts in mind: 1) "It is not my fault" (that I am the victim of a cultural conditioning process that promoted the learning of stereotypes); 2) "I can change" my knowledge base and belief system; and 3) "It is my ethical responsibility to change" (as a professional educator). Cognitive restructuring is the modification, changing, or restructuring of one's beliefs. A belief is what we perceive to be true and is a learned cognitive pattern. When a belief is erroneous, it can be unlearned to produce a newer, more accurate, and effective cognitive pattern. As more accurate cognitions replace the faulty or erroneous ones, changes in behavior will occur. Therefore, as old beliefs based on myths and stereotypes are replaced by a new set of beliefs, more culturally responsible behaviors will be developed.

Awareness is the key to becoming more culturally responsible in our interactions with African American students. Ultimately, we must experience a *CRI* or *Culturally Relevant Insight*. A CRI results when some event occurs that enables or forces us to deal at the conscious level with some previously unconscious belief. Sometimes, we gain these insights through attending a workshop; at other times, we are forced to confront our beliefs when we work with or become friends with someone about whom we previously held stereotypical beliefs. Hopefully, you will start to experience more CRIs after reading this book and completing the following four exercises. Because African Americans are most often involved in disciplinary referrals, the examples included in the awareness exercises are African American males.

Awareness Exercise #1

For each of the following stereotypes, list specific behaviors or actions that would indicate that you possibly hold beliefs about African American male students based on the stereotype. For example, if a teacher unconsciously believed that African American males were dishonest, he or she might automatically assume that when something in the classroom was missing, it was taken by an African American male. A teacher who held the beliefs that African American males were both intellectually inferior and dishonest might insist that an African American male student cheated when he made a good grade on a test.

STEREOTYPE BEHAVIOR/ACTION	TEACHER/ADMINISTRATOR BEHAVIOR/ACTION
Dishonest	
Aggressive/Violent	
Lazy	
Sexually Promiscuous	
Irresponsible	
Intellectually Inferior	
Dysfunctional Family	
Culturally Deprived	
Athletic	
Gang Member	

Ask yourself if, in any circumstances, you have demonstrated any of those behaviors or actions. Which of those behaviors or actions would or have students or parents felt that you demonstrated? If you are serious about this process, devise an anonymous method for your students to give you input regarding behaviors associated with each of the stereotypes. Finally, monitor your behaviors and actions. If the types of actions and behaviors you have listed occur, then spend some time reflecting on the possibly unconscious beliefs that you may hold about African American male students.

Awareness Exercise #2

Monitor your reactions to African American male students, especially when they are in groups, that is, walking down the corridor or sitting together in the cafeteria. When you feel a sense of fear, anger, or any discomfort, immediately ask yourself:

1. What am I thinking at this moment?
2. Is this thought related to a belief that I hold about African American males? What is the belief?
3. Is the belief connected to a myth or stereotype?
4. How does this thought influence my feelings and actions?

When time permits, again reflect on the thoughts and feelings you experienced. Ask yourself, "Can I honestly attribute the trait that made me feel uncomfortable to all African American male students? Why or why not? If all African American males are not the same, how can I change my beliefs and thoughts so that they are more objective and reflective of reality?" Practice identifying and refuting the erroneous beliefs when your feelings and actions indicate that they are operating at an unconscious level.

Awareness Exercise #3

Another activity that you can use to increase your ability to experience CRIs is to "replace the face." When you feel very annoyed, angered, or uncomfortable with the manner or actions of an African American male, visualize him with another face. Then ask yourself, "How would I respond if he were: not African American? not male? not poor?" Monitor your reactions to the mannerisms and actions of students who are not African American males. In what ways do you react to these students differently? Why?

Awareness Exercise #4

According to Kuykendall (1992), several factors can influence the way that teachers perceive and react to students. These are a student's 1) name, 2) gender, 3) socioeconomic status, 4) previous academic record (and records of siblings), 5) previous conduct record (and records of siblings), and 6) appearance. Poor African American males are placed in triple jeopardy of being the victim of negative perceptions, low expectations, and poor relationships with teachers. It has been my experience, and shared with me by other African American teachers, that when a student has a name like Jerome or Jamal, a not-so-good academic record, a few previous conflicts with a teacher, and he is very tall and very dark in complexion, he is at a very real risk of receiving a disciplinary referral and subsequent punishment. Take some time to reflect on the characteristics or profiles that cause you the most difficulty in establishing rapport or communicating effectively with an African American male student.

These exercises are designed to help you engage in a process that will make it easier to identify, confront, and change erroneous beliefs so that you can demonstrate more culturally responsive and responsible behaviors toward African American students.

RECOMMENDATIONS

Step #8: Practice cultural etiquette and apply the strategies for culturally effective management.

Do: Complete the Cognitive Restructuring Exercises.

CHAPTER 9

The Village Approach: Forming Partnerships with Parents and Community

In this book, I have primarily discussed the role and responsibility of the school in eliminating racial disparities in discipline. The research I have cited, my experiences as a race and gender consultant, and my discussions primarily with African American students, parents, teachers, administrators, and community members indicate that significant changes must be made in beliefs, attitudes, policies, and practices within the school setting if racial disparities in discipline are to be eliminated.

There is, however, a very definite role that African American parents and community members must play in reducing disciplinary referrals of African American students. Ask for the assistance of a core group of parents and community members. Be sure to include both adversaries and supporters, and individuals from all income strata.

FORMING A SCHOOL–COMMUNITY PARTNERSHIP

The first step in the process is to clarify the school's role and responsibility:

1. Ask for the assistance of the community in resolving the problem.
2. Acknowledge that there is a problem of racial disparity in discipline.
3. Acknowledge that the lack of cultural knowledge and unconscious stereotyping is a factor.
4. Make a commitment to take responsibility for changing the school climate.

Secondly, clarify the community's role and responsibility.

1. Express the expectation that the community will assist.
2. Try to involve ministers and express the desire that they take a leadership role in the process.
3. Express the expectation that knowledgeable community members will take a leadership role if it is difficult to recruit parents.
4. Expect ministers and community members to influence parents to be a part of the process.

Third, ask parents and community members to:

1. Provide mentors for troubled students.
2. Serve on a task force to design discipline policies.
3. Serve on a task force to develop criteria for placement in alternative programs.
4. Serve as members of a support team for students with discipline problems.
5. Serve on committees to define disciplinary offenses.
6. Serve on hearing panels for serious offenses.
7. Conduct classes for students related to traditional African American beliefs and values.

Finally, conduct dialogues with parents and community members about:

1. Their feelings related to race, racism, and bad experiences as a student.
2. Conflicts in parent and school values. For instance, fighting at school, even to defend oneself, is a punishable offense. Many African American parents, however, insist that their children "hit back" when hit. The child may even get into trouble at home for not defending himself. Many African American parents are authoritarian in their childrearing and believe in corporal punishment, that is, spanking or "whipping." Corporal punishment in most mainstream homes is taboo and even considered to be child abuse. Some African American parents feel that their rights as a

parent to discipline their children in a way that they feel is best have been taken away.

3. Provide information to:
    a. Parents and community members about the process for filing complaints or grievances.
    b. Teachers and administrators about African American culture and the issues that African American males face.
4. Provide support to:
    a. Single mothers and grandmothers raising children alone.
    b. Community groups who are willing to sponsor community-run programs for students with serious behavior problems. The strategies will be helpful in forming a partnership with parents and the community that will help increase communication, build trust, and provide a cooperative effort to decrease discipline problems.

RECOMMENDATIONS

Step #9: Initiate a partnership with parents and the community.
Do: Persist, even though the process may be slow.

CHAPTER 10

Evaluating the Process: School Climate and Individual Assessment

How do you know that the process you have undertaken to eliminate school-related factors that place African American male students at risk for disciplinary referrals and action is working? The most effective test is that you will see a decrease in the number of disciplinary referrals for African American students; if you are in a predominately African American school setting, you will see a decrease in disciplinary referrals in general. A by-product of this process can also be that you will have fewer complaints voiced and filed by African American parents. Very importantly, you will have created trust and a working partnership between the school and the community.

Creating an environment that is characterized by culturally responsive and culturally responsible behaviors is an ongoing process that will not only produce significant differences in the area of discipline but will influence the total school environment.

Evaluating the effectiveness of the change process involves conducting assessments at both the school climate and individual level. The first set of questions below involves an assessment of the school climate. The questions that follow relate not only to the disciplinary process but also to all aspects of the school culture. The questions will refer to "African American students"; if your school has a majority African American student population, rephrase the question to read, "African American students from lower socioeconomic backgrounds."

SCHOOL CLIMATE ASSESSMENT

Answer "yes" or "no" to each item. If you answer "yes" to an item, give specific examples to support your response.

1. Are high expectations (academic performance and social behavior) held for African American students?
2. Do African American students feel respected and accepted in the school environment?
3. Do African American students feel a sense of connectedness to the school community?
4. Is the language and culture of African American students respected and valued?
5. Are African American students free to express their cultural identity?
6. Do the formal and informal curricula include the accomplishments and contributions of Africans and African Americans?
7. Is creating a culturally sensitive and responsive school environment a school goal?
8. Is reducing the number of disciplinary referrals involving African American students, especially males, a priority issue?
9. Are disciplinary referrals for African American students, especially African American males, proportionate to their numbers in the school population?
10. Has a diverse committee (race, ethnicity, social class, teachers, students, parents, community members) been established to periodically review discipline policies and issues?
11. Have discipline policies and procedures been established that eliminate disparity related to race, gender, and social class?
12. Is disaggregated data (race, gender, social class) related to academic performance and discipline reviewed periodically?
13. Do instructional and resource materials have African American representation?
14. Does a representative number of African American students participate in all types of extracurricular activities?
15. Does a representative number of African American students hold leadership positions in student government and organizations?

16. Are African American students represented in all academic levels, for example, gifted, honors, etc., in proportion to their numbers in the school population?
17. Do teaching styles and assessment procedures reflect an understanding of the culture and experiences of African American students?
18. Do African American parents feel comfortable and welcome in the school environment?
19. Is the faculty comfortable interacting with African American parents?
20. Is the school's stated emphasis one of academic achievement rather than discipline and control?
21. Does discipline focus on teaching appropriate behavior as well as punishment?
22. Are all allegations of racism, sexism, and classism investigated?
23. Is ongoing professional development and technical assistance provided for faculty and staff related to cultural differences, stereotyping, discipline, etc.?
24. Is coaching provided for faculty members who have persistent problems with African American students?
25. Is coaching provided for faculty members who are resistant to the process of becoming more culturally responsive and responsible?
26. Is coaching provided for faculty members who receive a disproportionate number of persistent complaints from students and parents?
27. Are there sanctions against negative "lounge talk" about students?
28. Are culturally responsive and responsible behaviors included in the criteria for faculty evaluations and accountability?
29. Is hiring more African American and other faculty members of color a priority?
30. Is the climate assessment an ongoing process?

INDIVIDUAL ASSESSMENT

An assessment at the individual level will help teachers and administrators to know how they are progressing in terms of the process of becoming more culturally responsive and responsible. As was the case with the assessment of the school climate, affirmative responses given for the questions asked will indicate that the teacher or administrator has developed the beliefs and is demonstrating behaviors that make all students feel respected and valued.

Answer "yes" or "no" to each item. If you answer "yes" to an item, give specific examples to support your response.

1. Do I see the need to focus on the issues of groups of students who are experiencing difficulties, that is, African American males?
2. Am I open to participating in the process to develop more culturally responsive and responsible behaviors?
3. Am I willing to learn more about the culture of African American students?
4. Do I practice cultural etiquette as it relates to African American students?
5. Am I comfortable discussing issues related to race, culture, and social class?
6. Am I comfortable dealing with issues related to race, culture, and social class?
7. Am I effective in dealing with issues related to race, culture, and social class?
8. Do I monitor my own behavior to be sure that I am not reacting on the basis on unconscious stereotyping?
9. Do I work to establish rapport and build effective relationships with African American students?
10. Have I set a goal for reducing disciplinary referrals involving African American male students?
11. Do I understand my own power issues and find "win–win" ways to gain the respect of students?
12. Have I overcome my fear of African American males?
13. Do I seek the advice of other colleagues when I am experiencing difficulty with a particular student?
14. Do I seek to understand the motivation for student misbehavior?
15. When I have persistent conflict with a student, do I:
    a. seek to dialogue with the student?
    b. examine my own beliefs and behaviors?

    c. take seriously any comment made by the student about feeling that he is the victim of racism, prejudice, etc., and seek to discover why he feels this way?

16. Do I allow students who have misbehaved to "start anew"?
17. Do I seek input from students regarding classroom rules and issues related to discipline?
18. Do I, to the best of my ability, try to see the world through the "eyes of my students"?
19. Have I made a commitment to be more effective in relating to and communicating with African American males?
20. Do I handle "nonserious" disciplinary issues in my classroom?
21. Do I examine the "precipitating factors" when an incident occurs?
22. Am I aware of my beliefs and behaviors that cause an incident to escalate?
23. Am I aware of my beliefs and behaviors that facilitate establishing good relationships with African American male students?
24. Am I aware of my beliefs and behaviors that hinder my establishing good relationships with African American male students?
25. Do I "see and respect" color (differences)?
26. Do I seek to dialogue with parents about student misbehavior before it reaches a serious level?
27. Am I willing to engage in conflict resolution with a student?
28. Do I always conduct myself in a professional and ethical manner with students?
29. Do I take advantage of "teachable moments" to help students understand why certain behavior is inappropriate?
30. Do I engage in an ongoing process of reflection and self-assessment?

The climate and individual assessments were designed to serve as an indicator of the extent to which new belief systems and modes of behavior are being instituted in the school environment. They provide a measure of the type of changes that individual teachers and administrators are making as well as the impact these changes have on the total school culture.

CONCLUSION

Culturally responsible actions are those that ensure students will not receive disparate treatment as a result of conscious or unconscious bias or prejudices. In this instance, culturally responsible actions are those taken to prevent African American students from being the victims of historical myths and stereotypes. This change is based on the recognition that stereotypical images of African American males, in particular, are both persistent and pervasive. They are also perpetuated through a cultural conditioning process from which teachers are not immune.

Stereotyping is a sensitive issue that many teachers and administrators find very difficult to acknowledge and talk about. The mere mention of the word "stereotype" often brings about immediate denials, defensiveness, and the "I am the exception syndrome," where individuals seek to prove that they remained untouched by cultural conditioning process.

At the institutional or school climate level, changes that relate to cultural responsiveness involve professional development and modifications in school practices so that students are not penalized for cultural differences. Changes related to cultural responsibility include a system of teacher accountability and evaluation that emphasizes the teacher's ability to demonstrate culturally sensitive and responsive behaviors toward all students.

At the individual level, cultural responsiveness involves the practice of cultural etiquette or social forms that respect the preferences and taboos of cultural groups. Changes related to cultural responsibility will involve cognitive restructuring, a process of modifying beliefs that are based on historical myths and stereotypes.

It is imperative that we give our attention to what is happening to African American students. The disciplinary process as it is currently implemented has almost predictable outcomes, all of which are negative and place young African American males especially at risk for negative consequences in the larger society. We are losing far too many of these young men. It is time that we examine the issues again and try some new approaches. The one thing that we do know is that something is desperately wrong and that what we have done in the past and are doing currently is not working.

I offer this book as another way to view the problem. We have spent more money and time imaginable trying to "fix students" and their parents while ignoring some core social problems in this society that affect our schools, just as they do every other institution in America. We have gone about as far as we can with the "blame the victim" paradigm. It is time to honestly face ourselves, to make some fundamental changes, and to make our schools places of emotional as well as physical safety. No student should be the victim of the harm that results from ignorance of his culture or the stigma imposed by historical images.

RECOMMENDATIONS

Step #10: Make maintaining equity in discipline a school priority.
Do: Remember that equity ensures excellence!

Appendix: The African American Male School Experience

An item that I often include on a beliefs survey when I conduct workshops with teachers and administrators is: *All students, regardless of racial, cultural, or social class background have the same* in-school *learning opportunities.* I always emphasize the "in-school" experience, and ask the participants not to think of anything but what happens to the student after he sets foot on the school grounds. Initially, many participants will agree that all students have the same and equal opportunities to learn in the school setting. Some even suggest that since minority and poor students often attend schools or participate in programs that receive large amounts of federal aid, they actually have greater learning opportunities than other students.

After some discussion and reflection, however, there is usually agreement that all students do not have the same learning opportunities in the school setting. Students have the same status and experiences in our schools as they have in the larger society, of which the school is a microcosm. Students who belong to stigmatized groups in the larger society belong to stigmatized groups in our schools. African American males are a stigmatized group within the larger American society, and African American male students belong to a stigmatized group in most school settings.

The moment of greatest opportunity for any student is when he or she is interacting with his or her teacher. Students who belong to stigmatized groups do not have the same interactions with their teachers as their more privileged peers. When a student is feared, believed to be of poor moral character, or believed to be intellectually inferior, it is difficult for him to have interactions that provide him with the fullest opportunity to excel as a student.

What is it like to be an African American male student? Given the lack of understanding of his culture, the disdain for his mannerisms, and the misperceptions about him, it is likely not to be a very pleasant experience. Often, he does not understand why he is disliked or feared, or why so little is expected and thought of him. He feels powerless to change any of the feelings and opinions that are held of him. He only knows that he must constantly be on guard.

When I inquired of African American male teachers what it is like to be the victim of myths and stereotypes, they had some very strong and definite feelings. There comments are summarized below.

"It hurts."

"It's sad."

"No matter what you do, nothing changes."

"I'm tired of proving myself."

"You hold it in."

"It's not fair."

"I'm always prepared to challenge."

"I'm not a bad person."

"I get angry."

The response heard most often from the group was that they became angry. Anger, in fact, is the most common human response to a sense of powerlessness. We encounter very angry African American male students each day; some of the anger stems from their view of their place in the world, some is their response to bad home situations, and some comes from the sense of frustration and powerlessness that they feel in the school setting. This anger is turned either inward or outward. When the anger is turned inward, we find African American male students who are depressed, who suffer from psychosomatic ills, who abuse alcohol and drugs, who engage in reckless and self-destructive behaviors, and some who—in increasing numbers—commit suicide.

When young African American males direct the anger outward (which is a common human behavior resulting from the sense of powerlessness), they engage in aggressive and violent behavior. Much of the aggressive behavior that we see directed toward teachers comes from this sense of powerlessness. Many conflicts between African American males and teachers result from power struggles or the student's perception of the abuse of power. Stereotyping, conscious or unconscious, produces a sense of powerlessness in the African American male, and subsequently leads to conflict. Creating a school culture, in which the culture of the African American male is respected and where stereotyping is not tolerated, will help to decrease both the anger and the aggressive behavior so often seen in young African American males.

Bibliography

Advancement Project and Civil Rights Project. "Opportunities Suspended: The Devastating Consequences of Zero Tolerance and School Discipline." (Washington, D.C.: Advancement Project; Cambridge, Mass.: Harvard University, Civil Rights Project, 2000).

Althen, G. *American Ways: A Guide for Foreigners in the United States.* (Yarmouth, Maine: Intercultural Press, 1988).

Applied Research Center. "Facing the Consequences: An Examination of Racial Discrimination in U.S. Public Schools." ERASE Report (Oakland, Calif.: Applied Research Center, ERASE Initiative, 2000).

Atkinson, D., G. Morten, and D. Sue. *Counseling American Minorities: A Cross-cultural Perspective,* 2nd ed. (Dubuque, Iowa: William C. Brown, 1983).

Bireda, M. "The Mythical African American Male," WEEA Digest (Newton, Mass.: WEEA Resource Center, 2000).

Boskin, J. "The National Jester in the Popular Culture." In *The Great Fear,* ed. Gary Nash and Richard Weiss. (New York: Holt, Rinehart, and Winston, 1970), 165–85.

———. *The Rise and Demise of an American Jester.* (New York: Oxford University Press, 1986).

Butler, J. P. "Of Kindred Minds: The Ties That Bind." In *Cultural Competence for Educators,* ed. Mario A. Orlandi. (Rockville, Md.: U.S. Department of Health and Human Services, 1992), 23–54.

Children's Defense Fund. "Children Out of School in America" (Washington, D.C.: Children's Defense Fund of the Washington Research Report).

Dandy, E. B. *Black Communication: Breaking Down the Barriers.* (Chicago, Ill.: African American Images, 1991).

Eyler, J., V. Cook, and L. Ward. "Resegregation: Segregation within Desegregated Schools." In *The Consequences of School Desegregation*, ed. Christine Rossell and Willis D. Hawley (Philadelphia, Pa.: Temple University Press, 1983).

Glasser, William. *Control Theory in the Classroom*. (New York: Harper Row, 1986).

Greenfield, P. M., C. Raeff, and B. Quiroz. "Cultural Values in Learning and Education." In *Closing the Achievement Gap: A Vision for Changing Beliefs and Practices*, ed. Belinda Ho (Arlington, Va.: Association for Supervision and Curriculum Development, 1996), 37–55.

Hale-Benson, J. E. *Black Children: Their Roots, Culture, and Learning Styles*. (Baltimore, Md.: John Hopkins University Press, 1986).

Herskovits, M. J., *The Myth of the Negro Past*. (Boston: Beacon Press, 1958).

Hillard, A. "Alternatives to IQ Testing: An Approach to the Identification of Gifted Minority Children." In *Black Children: Their Roots, Culture, and Learning Styles* by J. E. Benson (Baltimore, Md.: John Hopkins University Press, 1986), 43.

Ho, M. K. *Family Therapy with Ethnic Minorities*. (Newbury, Calif.: Sage, 1987).

Hodgkinson, H. *Secondary Schools in a New Millennium: Demographic Certainties, Social Realities*. (Reston, Va.: National Association of Secondary School Principals, 2000).

Hyman, I. A., and P. A. Snook. *Dangerous Schools: What We Can Do about the Physical and Emotional Abuse of Our Children*. (San Francisco, Calif.: Jossey-Bass Publishers, 1999).

Johnston, R. "Federal Data Highlight Disparities in Discipline." *Education News* (June 21, 2000).

Joint Center for Political Studies. *Visions of a Better Way: A Black Appraisal of Public Schooling*. (Washington, D.C.: Joint Center for Political Studies Press, 1989).

Kuykendall, C. *From Rage to Hope: Strategies for Reclaiming Black and Hispanic Students*. (Bloomington, Ind.: National Educational Service, 1992).

Locke, D. C. *Increasing Multicultural Understanding: A Comprehensive Model*. (Newbury Park, Calif.: Sage, 1992).

Loewenberg, P. "The Psychology of Racism." In *The Great Fear*, ed. Gary Nash and Richard Weiss (New York: Holt, Rinehart, & Winston, 1970).

Lynch, E. W., and M. J. Hanson. *Developing Cross-cultural Competence: A Guide for Working with Young Children and Their Families*. (Baltimore, Md.: Paul H. Brookes Publishing, 1992).

Meirer, K., J. Stewart, and R. England. *Race, Class, and Education: The Politics of Second-Generation Discrimination.* (Madison: University of Wisconsin Press, 1989).

Newby, I. A. *Jim Crow's Defense: Anti-Negro Thought in America 1900–1930.* (Baton Rouge: Louisiana State University, 1965).

Office of Civil Rights. *Student Discipline.* (Washington, D.C.: HEW Fact Sheet, 1974).

———. *Racial Incidents and Harassment against Students at Educational Institutional Guidance*, no. 59. (Washington, D.C.: Federal Register 11448, 10 March 1994).

———. *Proactive Docket Activities—Fiscal Year 2001.* (Atlanta, Ga.: Southern Division, 2001).

Ogbu, J. *Minority Education and Caste: The American System in Cross-cultural Perspective.* (New York: Academic Press, 1978).

Oliver, W. "Reflections on Manhood." In *Images of Color: Images of Crime,* ed. Coramae Mann and Marjorie Zatz (Los Angeles, Calif.: Roxbury, 1998), 81.

Paul, A. M. "Where Bias Begins: The Truth about Stereotypes," *Psychology Today* 31 (May/June 1998), 52–56.

Peretti, P. O. "Effects of Teacher's Attitudes on Discipline Problems in Schools Recently Desegregated." In *The Consequences of School Desegregation,* ed. Christine Rossell and Willis Hawley (Philadelphia, Pa.: Temple University Press, 1983).

Reddick, L. D. "The Nineteen Basic Stereotypes of Blacks in American Society." *Journal of Negro Education* 12 (1944).

Rome, D. "Stereotyping by the Media: Murderers, Rapists, and Drug Addicts." In *Images of Color: Images of Crime,* ed. Coramae Mann and Marjorie Zatz (Los Angeles, Calif.: Roxbury, 1998), 86–87.

Skiba, R. J., R. S. Michael, A. C. Nardo, and R. Peterson. *The Color of Discipline: Sources of Racial Gender Disproportionality in School Punishment.* (Bloomington: University of Indiana Education Policy Center, 2000).

Sobel, M. *The World They Made Together: Black and White Values in Eighteenth-Century Virginia.* (Princeton, N.J.: Princeton University Press, 1987).

Willis, W. "Families with African American Roots." In *Developing Cross-cultural Competence: A Guide for Working with Young Children and Their Families,* ed. E. W. Lynch and M. J. Hanson (Baltimore, Md.: Paul H. Brookes, 1992).

Wynn, C. "Black and White Bibb County Classrooms." In *The Consequences of School Desegregation*, ed. Christine Rossell and Willis Hawley (Philadelphia, Penn.: Temple University Press, 1983), 145.

Zuniga, M. "Families with Latino Roots." In *Developing Cross-cultural Competence: A Guide for Working with Young Children and Their Families,* ed. E. W. Lynch and M. J. Hanson (Baltimore, Md.: Paul H. Brookes, 1992).